Practising Reiki

MIND • BODY • AND SPIRIT

Practising Reiki

MIND · BODY · AND SPIRIT

Jennie Austin

LUCEM LIBRIS
DISSEMINAMUS

GEDDES & GROSSET

This edition published 2008 by Geddes & Grosset,
David Dale House, New Lanark, ML11 9DJ, Scotland

First published 1999
Reprinted 2002, 2004, 2007

© 1999 Geddes & Grosset

ISBN 978 1 84205 613 4

Printed and bound in the UK

Contents

Warning

Please note:

The author is not medically trained or qualified and neither she nor the publisher take responsibility for the application of the methods described in this book.

Reiki should never be used in place of medical treatment and care.

You should never stop taking or reduce any medication without consulting your doctor.

Fasting or any drastic change in diet should not be undertaken without the advice of your doctor.

Be aware that Reiki can reduce pain and symptoms, and, if going to a doctor, this may hinder accuracy in their diagnosis.

By law, children and animals must receive adequate medical care. Reiki does not count as such, so if either is ill, make sure that they get appropriate medical treatment. Reiki can, however, be used to complement any orthodox treatment received.

June Woods' Foreword

I am delighted to write a few words for this publication. As Jennie's Master/Teacher, I had the privilege of initiating her to the Reiki Second and Third Master Degree levels of this wonderfully simple healing process. So many books have been written from many different pathways of training. We have often discussed the need for a very simple form of book that would be clearly understood by the general public – to inform the many who are now forming an interest in alternative therapies. Everyone has the potential to become a healing channel for this beautiful *universal energy*, and has the basic requirements to attain this. Jennie herself is a dedicated therapist with many skills learnt over many years, including aromatherapy, reflexology, Bach flower remedies and electro-crystal therapy, but, as she says, the Reiki energy is present within *any* other form of healing. When you have received the initiations, this energy is always within you, for self-healing and as a channel to share with others. You will hear of the many results that have been of benefit to those who have received a healing session from those who have committed to helping their fellow beings. With love and blessings,

June Woods

Reiki Master

Foreword to this Edition

Welcome to the bigger edition of *Practising Reiki*. It is ten years since I tapped out *Practising Reiki* on my computer. Since then the world has changed and evolved at an amazing speed and Reiki has not been left behind. Back then there was very little information in the West and, what there was, was passed on by a scattering of Masters and a few books. Now there is an abundance of Teaching Masters and shelves in shops creak under the weight of books covering a huge range of approaches. These have come about through mankind's ability to imagine and manifest.

Practising Reiki still offers the basics, and I trust that it will continue to provide the foundations for those to come, to inspire them to imagine and manifest to keep up with the need for Reiki on our planet and for its inhabitants.

I would like to thank all those who have taken time to write to me and apologies if you had to wait for an answer. Also thanks to all the Master Teachers who have chosen to give copies of *Practising Reiki* to their students and to those who have taken it worldwide.

I now have a website (*see* page 27) where you can keep up with developments and find my up-to-date contact details.

The blessings of Reiki to you, with love,

Jennie Austin

Reiki Master

Introduction

This book does not set out to be a definitive work on Reiki, but is an introductory guide. It is a starting place, a place of introduction. Reiki is a constant, yet its presentation comes in diverse forms as do the humans that work with it. My aim is to present a taster of some of the options, and hope that, for those who know nothing about it, it will inspire them to join the many who are already benefiting from Reiki. It will perhaps set them on their way to finding the path that suits them. For those who already know Reiki, I hope many will find what I have written pleasing. If they don't, I hope that it offers them a view of wider horizons while clarifying and reinforcing their personal expression of Reiki.

Reading this book, and working with the methods and sequences within, does not enable you to channel Reiki. To do this you need to be trained and attuned by a Master. But don't let this put you off. There are many Masters and training centres about and the training is not difficult. We all have to start somewhere, and if this book is your first contact with Reiki, may I welcome you wholeheartedly and hope that you will benefit from Reiki as much as I have and continue to do, whether as a patient or as an initiated Reiki-ist.

To you all, happy reading, and the blessings of Reiki,

Jennie Austin

Reiki Master

A Personal View

I have been working with complementary therapies since 1983, when I came to them initially as a patient, and being so impressed with their approach and effects I went on over the years to qualify in aromatherapy, reflexology, electro-crystal therapy, the Bach flower remedies, and to study in-depth shiatsu, hypnotherapy, radionics, counselling, nutrition and Feng Shui. When I realised the massive potential of these therapies, especially in the areas of self-help, I decided to train as a Teacher. Since I qualified I have taught many people how to use these therapies for themselves, their friends and family, and some to work professionally. This has been a privilege and has brought me much satisfaction and fulfilment for which I give unending thanks.

As I explored various therapies I became aware of the importance of vibrational energies – the invisible energies, that mystics have always known were there, but that science could not quantify and so did not acknowledge. As science is growing up (it is only a baby really as far as time is concerned), it too is acknowledging that there is more to us, life, our planet etc, than purely empirical things and forces that can be registered on instruments.

Reiki joined me on my path of life in 1988. Like so many others I came upon it by chance. (Is there such a thing as chance?) I saw an advert in the local newspaper for a talk. I went, not knowing what Reiki was but feeling an undeniable urge to attend. By the weekend I had been initiated into the

Practising Reiki

First Degree of Reiki. I never questioned my unsubstantiated decision to do the course, there really did not seem to be any need to. I just *knew* that it was my next step.

It did not make massive changes in my life. It did not rock the universe for me – yet, in hindsight, I can see how the pace and character of my life altered. It carried me through change, supported me during what was already a very stressful time, and supplied me with insights that made even the challenges fulfilling. I like to have proof, and although I wanted to believe Reiki could be all that was suggested on the course, I was at that time not allowing my sensitivity a free rein. It all seemed too good to be true. I had been raised in an atmosphere of discipline and tangible fact, and of not challenging my elders and betters. Reiki was a bit far out of the accepted format, it seemed to defy logic, yet for me it manifested all my childhood suspicions that there was more to life than we were being told about. I mixed with people who implied that if I was any sort of a therapist or healer, then I didn't need to have Reiki. So I went underground with my Reiki. I trundled on, on the face of it working without Reiki, yet adding Reiki to everything that I did, using both belt and braces. Any good effects it might have had were met with the response: 'Well, that might have happened anyway!'

My 'betters'(?) were telling me that it didn't count, so who was I to challenge them? I continued to give Reiki the benefit of the doubt, applying Reiki energy here, there and anywhere just in case Reiki was really working. I – though I should say we (Reiki and I) – had successes, but if you are a doubting Thomas it is surprising how you can explain things away.

Then, Cathleen, a neighbour, said she was going to do Reiki. Her enthusiasm was contagious. At last someone that I respected had confirmed what I believed in. I started to be more diligent about my self-treatments, and found they made such a difference that I wanted to kick myself for having allowed myself to be influenced by others, and having wasted several years not benefiting from Reiki as much as I could have. I still had no desire to progress to the Second Degree, finding the First Degree wonderful to use in my work as a complementary health practitioner, especially now that I had 'come out'. However, I was not to be allowed to stand still. Cathleen was so impressed with Reiki that she went on to do her Second Degree. Then she asked me to work with her and another friend in a healing centre, which I eagerly agreed to do. That was when I found I could no longer leave Reiki on the back burner. At this point I was still not interested in going any further in my training (which is not like me; I usually like the challenge of things new with little patience for having to wait). However, I believe that this slow progression stood me in good stead, and that the slow assimilation of Reiki has given me a deep knowledge and experience of it, that I would not have got had I rushed into it.

Finally, in 1994, a Second-Degree training weekend came up, and I couldn't find an excuse for not doing it. My First-Degree initiation had been so subtle, that at the time I sensed nothing, and just had to accept my Master's word that it had worked. It is only in hindsight that I can recognise its full impact. But my Second Degree nearly blew my socks off! It was all the more astounding as I had not had any expectations. Of course I then went into overdrive, and wanted to be a Master. Already being a Teacher, I wanted to share this with others, and now I thank my Master, June Woods, for her wisdom, as despite my nagging, whingeing, feeling hard done by, and threats of finding another Master who would initiate me, she advised me to wait. Eventually just over a year later, she initiated me – and of course the time was just right. The bonus was that I learnt the importance of correct timing and along with this some patience.

Although I am a practitioner of several holistic disciplines,

Practising Reiki

I find that people are attracted to Reiki like bees to a beautifully scented flower. Often the other therapies are the initial contact, but then they will say something like 'What's this Reiki stuff?' and before I know it they're wanting Reiki as well as, or instead of their initial choice of treatment or training. Even when I give talks on other therapies, at question time, more often than not, someone will want to know about Reiki, even though I have not mentioned it verbally and it is just a line or two on my information leaflet. People will phone me, not knowing what Reiki is, but saying that it keeps coming to their notice, and they ask when can they come and be trained. Many of these people are logical, practical and very grounded people and who for no reason that they can find are drawn instinctively to this blessed energy.

Reiki is a bit like having a good friend who is always there for you. I don't think I have ever had a situation when Reiki has not been there to help and improve it. Life doesn't suddenly become a bed of roses with Reiki, but it helps to smooth the corners and often helps us to see the answers that so often elude us. It has probably been the thing in my life that has made the biggest impact. My life is better for Reiki, and I cannot imagine being without it. I hope that after you have read this book, you will have some idea of why I am so enthusiastic about it.

I have been blessed with a peaceful patch in the beautiful Highlands of Scotland, where I can grow, teach and treat – working with humans, animals and nature. If you would like to get in touch, I would be happy to hear from you. I will answer all communications, but please be patient when waiting for replies as we experience a cycle with periods of intense activity, when we hardly have time to sleep, alternating with times of almost total inertia, during which we recover, and prepare for the next spell of challenges and opportunities. The speed of reply will depend on when you contact us.

If you wish to contact me, please do so via my website which gives all my contact details:

www.jennieaustin.com

Those requesting distance healing will receive it as soon as possible after the contact is made.

Definitions

The following define my use of these particular words in this publication:

- **attunement** – part of the initiation process. It is the action that enables the student to channel the Reiki. Once attuned, the enablement is for life. However, there is the choice to use it or not.
- **Degree** – in most traditions there are three. They are the different levels of training. *See* **Training**.
- **dis-ease** – the manifestation of a state when the mind, body and spirit are not in harmony, either within each or between one another, and therefore dis-ease is created.
- **form** – the method of Reiki taught to students that they will use as a base for their PRACTICE.
- **healee** – the person having a Reiki treatment.
- **healer** – the term often used to describe a person who channels Reiki. This is a misnomer, as the 'healer' does not heal anyone! However, this person does facilitate the transfer of the Reiki energy, putting it there for the healee to draw on. The healee is really the healer! It is the healee's own healing system that does the job. Reiki helps by fuelling it with the vital life force needed. Instead of 'healer' I will use the word Reiki-ist.
- **initiation** – this is the process that enables a person to work with Reiki. It includes attunements, training and information.
- **Master** – in Reiki this is a person who has been initiated

into the Third Degree. Masters have also been given the methods and instruction to enable them to initiate others to Reiki. However some Third-Degree initiates choose not to teach and initiate. *See* chapter on Masters.

- **Reiki-ist** – this is a person who has been initiated to use Reiki. Often misnamed as a HEALER.
- **practice** – the way in which a Reiki-ist personally works with Reiki. It is based on the form taught by their Master.
- **transition** – the voyage from this life to the afterlife
- **TLC** – tender loving care.
- **wellness** – this is a state of *good* health, it is not just a lack of symptoms. A person who is well should be full of beans and full of enthusiasm for the day ahead.

What is Reiki and What is it Not?

A hands-on healing technique

A Reiki treatment combines the utilisation of the universal life energy with the warmth, reassurance, and healing power of human touch.

Reiki is most popularly known as a hands-on healing technique. However, it can also become an integral part of life for those who have been initiated. It helps with health problems, but this is only a small part of its wondrous attributes. It can help in just about any area of your life that you would like it to.

The word Reiki, literally translated, means 'Universal Life Force' and this is exactly what it is. It is everywhere, limitless, abundant, ecological, environmentally friendly, cruelty-free, cost-effective, suitable for vegans, vegetarians, carnivores, and available to anyone who has been attuned to access it. The attunements process which is instigated by an initiated Master is like tuning a radio set to pick up a particular station. Please note that there are other healing rays that can be accessed by non initiated persons. To use this particular ray you *must* have been attuned to do so. Spiritual healers that have been initiated to Reiki say that the different energies have their own feel to them.

Reiki, although not called that in times long past, was part of a whole that included healing techniques and self awareness, development, growth and means of living life in harmony and happiness, (*see* **Reiki Principles**). To work with this system does not require you to believe or to be greatly skilled. However, a desire to work with it is necessary and dedicated practice enhances the results. The self-treatment is paramount in the development of the Reiki-initiated person, and is a deceptively simple way of growing and benefiting on all levels – i.e. mentally, physically, emotionally and spiritually.

Spiritual but not religious

It is important not to get the concept of spirituality mixed with that of religion. Reiki does not tie into any particular religion. People of all sorts of belief systems and cultures are initiated into Reiki and benefit from it daily. In many cultures today, this link with our own spirituality and the Divine/Almighty/Goddess/God/Great Spirit/Higher Self – whatever you choose to call it – has been lost. The loss of this natural and necessary link has caused many problems that we can see around us. It is a bit like trying to make a cake without the flour, it doesn't quite work out right. You do not have to contribute to this view to benefit from Reiki. I have initiated some confirmed sceptics. Some have maintained their views and worked well with Reiki, while others have surprised themselves and now wonder how they could have existed without this connection after Reiki has assisted them to reconnect.

Reiki energy – a vital life force

Reiki is a specific energy that helps our own healing systems to work to their full potential. It helps us to vitalise and balance. The word healer, which is often used to describe Reiki-enabled people, implies that *they* do the healing. This is not so. I feel wary about using this term, as it can inflate the ego. I prefer to use the term *Reiki-ist* instead, because what they do is access and facilitate the transfer of the Reiki, presenting it for the patient/healee to draw upon, and control the flow themselves. This is not usually done consciously, most people would choose to be well, so it is practically an automatic facilitation. The Reiki then fills them with vital life force that fuels their own healing system, enabling it to work more efficiently.

Healing

When we think of healing, we usually assume this means the ridding of symptoms and illness. However, healing should be considered on all levels (mind, emotions, body, spirit) because a lack of harmony on any level or discord between levels will cause imbalance, and eventually illness and symptoms somewhere in the whole. It is possible to fend off this eventuality by bringing back the overall harmony to that whole. Reiki can help here. When dealing with symptoms it is worth remembering that many physical ailments are only manifestations of long-term imbalances within the total person, and that the ailment is a final cry for help. This is why a person needs to be viewed in completeness, consisting of the various parts, not the parts in isolation. If it is only the symptom that is removed, the cause will only send up another cry for help, possibly moving the symptom to another location, or refusing to respond to treatment.

Reiki is simplicity itself, and this sometimes belies its effectiveness. Particularly in the West where we like things that are technical, that can be proved, have huge instruction manuals and work fast. The basics of Reiki can be learned in a weekend, and from the moment of attunement the Reiki-ist can use Reiki, though it takes different individuals varying lengths of time to fully assimilate the energies. This happens naturally and is aided by constant and regular use of Reiki. It is not easy to put Reiki into words. It is only fairly recently that we have been able to show graphically what happens, for instance with Kirlian photography and Harry Oldfield's PIP scans. Both of these methods photograph the energy fields of the body rather than only the physical.

The three Degrees of Reiki

Reiki is taught in three levels or Degrees. Some lineages have divided it into more though the content remains largely the same. These levels must be completed in order, though not all have to be done to use Reiki.

The First Degree or Reiki I

The First Degree is primarily for the self. I hear some saying that this is selfish, but I would like to quote the Knights Templar: 'work on yourself and serve the world.' So many of us feel that we must put others first all the time, but sometimes it comes to the point that, because we have not cared for ourselves, we cannot give of our best to others either. The First Degree also teaches methods for treating others, with hands-on healing for use on friends and family.

The Second Degree or Reiki II

The Second Degree is often looked on as the practitioner level, i.e. it passes on the Sacred Symbols that enable the person to access and focus Reiki in a more powerful way, and also to use Reiki for distance healing. Most Masters do not teach the mundane practicalities of functioning and working as a professional practitioner, only the advanced Reiki skills. I have added a few notes on some of the things that potential Reiki practitioners must consider if they start their own business in **Guidelines for Being a Practitioner**.

The Third Degree or Reiki III

The Third Degree is for those who have made a deep commitment to Reiki, using it in their lives. The full Third-Degree initiation enables them to initiate others to use Reiki, and to work with the Master energies. Not all those who are attuned to the Third Degree teach, some just work with the higher levels of energy. There is a very wide spectrum of training offered by Masters, and indeed in the training that Masters have received.

See more on the form of classes in **Reiki Training**.

Lineages

In Reiki there are lineages. These are like family trees. They trace the flow of initiations from Master to Master to student. There are a number of different lineages in Reiki, but all should start with Dr Mikaomi Usui, as he is the founder of Reiki.

Money and energy exchanges have varying Degrees of importance and interpretation in different lineages and I have covered this in a chapter on its own.

Reiki is versatile

Reiki can enhance all sorts of areas in your life. They include self development and awareness, support and maintenance of wellbeing and health for the self and others, children, animals and plants. It can be of help with first aid (though not instead of medical care in the case of emergencies), cooking, gardening, fear, stress, dying, in the home, work, hospitals and hospices, and for healing the past, assisting the present and helping the future. It can also serve well in support of other healing modalities, both orthodox and alternative. If used with common sense it is safe and effective.

What Reiki is not:

- Reiki is not a replacement for medical treatment.
- Reiki is not a cure all.
- Reiki is not a cult or weird sect.
- Reiki is not just a therapy.

Questions and Answers

Here are some questions that have been asked about Reiki. The answers should help to dispel some of the inaccuracies, myths and old wives' tales.

Is Reiki a cult or a secret society? Once I have been initiated will I be tied for life?

No. Reiki is not a cult or a secret society. There is a large body of like-minded people who try to live by the principles set out in Reiki. These are not rules, but suggestions for making life a more fulfilling and happy experience (*see* **Reiki Principles**). Once you have been initiated you have complete responsibility for how you use Reiki, if at all. You will have the ability there for you whenever you want to use it, instantaneously, but it is your decision. It is hoped that you will *want* to live the Reiki principals and to use Reiki to enhance every area of your life.

If Reiki is misused will something awful happen?

Unlikely! It is more likely that nothing will happen at all and that it will not aid the misuse. However, what reaction the misuse itself may invoke will depend on the misuse itself.

What happens if someone who is not initiated tries to use the Sacred Symbols?

Again, nothing. Only those that have been attuned to use the symbols can activate them. Others may think by the power of thought that they can use them, but they could probably do just the same if they had a picture of Mickey Mouse and believed that it was a Sacred Symbol. The power of thought is very strong, and can have powerful results, but use of the Reiki Sacred Symbols as they were intended requires that the person using them has been attuned to their vibrations.

After a Reiki treatment, sometimes healees experience:
a) a worsening in their condition,
b) a past illness reappearing, or
c) they get a headache, a runny nose, a need to go to the toilet more, or just feel tired. Why is this?

a) The Reiki boosts the person's own healing system and this often goes into overdrive in order to combat the problem. This causes a momentary overcompensation and so the symptoms may temporally get worse.

b) A past illness may reappear, as it has not really been 'cured'. It may well have only be suppressed either by drugs or by the healees themselves so that they can get on with life as best they can. Reiki gets to the root of the problem and starts the process from there, thus releasing the symptoms and then helping in the healing. This often happens with emotions. It is not always necessary to know the cause to enable the illness or emotion to be healed.

c) These are all symptoms of detoxification. In response to the Reiki the body clears out the 'rubbish', using the evacuation routes, such as the bowel and nose. Headaches are also a part of the detoxification. Feeling tired is usually because the body is using all its available energy to do this 'detoxing' and then regeneration. It is wise to rest if possible, and let this process proceed. Energy levels usually improve after it is completed. Some people experience extra energy after treatments.

Why does Reiki sometimes work so slowly in comparison with orthodox medicine?

Reiki and some of the orthodox cures work in different ways. Reiki heals starting with the cause, whereas quite often orthodox medicine will start by getting rid of the symptom, and sometimes leaves it at that. Reiki works at a gentle pace, easing the body through the change from *dis-ease* (*see* **Definitions**) to balance. Reiki does sometimes work at a surprisingly speedy pace, this is whcn it feels as though there has been a minor miracle. It is also beneficial in easing the discomfort of symptoms, but it is, at the same time, working on the cause.

Why doesn't Reiki always work?

More often than not Reiki will bring about some form of improvement. However there are three reasons why no improvement might be seen.

One is that a person might have an investment in the illness, and although he or she goes through all the motions of attempting to get well, there is an underlying reluctance to be truly well. This may not be a conscious thing – let me explain. People who are ill will often be treated with more tolerance than people who have no reason for being awkward, bad tempered, demanding, etc, and they can get their own way more often. People who need help to do things, can command people's time and company. Some people may also feel unworthy of attention in their own right, and find that illness fills the gap.

Others are not ready to be well. Illness and disease are great teachers. How many people have said that after a near call from death or a serious illness, that their whole outlook on life has changed? Illness can present us with experiences and lessons that we would not have encountered had we not been afflicted.

Sometimes the person's illness is too far advanced on a

physical level. But, as I said, usually some benefit is experienced.

Can Reiki turn people mad?

No. However, people who have a mental problem would be best to sort it out before becoming initiated, as the swing from their out-of-balance state to the heightened one often experiences after initiations could be more than they can comfortably cope with or understand.

It is advisable for some people to allow a period of time between different Degrees, as taking them one after another can cause quite a swing in the energies. Even a single Degree can make you feel very different. This should be talked through with the initiating Master.

If you give Reiki to dying people you will kill them. Is this true?

Who can say when people will die – even if they have been labelled as terminal. I have been called in to treat someone who is not expected to last the night, only to visit the next day and find them sitting up eating their lunch and smiling happily. This question was asked of me by someone who had asked someone to send Reiki for her father who was 'terminally ill'. I was concerned that she had been told that the Reiki would kill him.

I prefer to think that if his last moments were pain-free and coherent, this is preferable to living them out in distress. I believe that Reiki helps remove the fear of death, and that it aids the person to pass consciously and with dignity, at the time that is right for them. It does not push them on their way.

Those who have not been initiated to Reiki by a 'proper' Master will get paralysed from the waist down. Is this true?

Reiki is not vindictive. You will come to no harm through the channelling of Reiki – it is loving and benevolent. If the person is unable to channel the Reiki then it is more likely that nothing will happen.

If a Master channelled some other energy, that was not Reiki, then I could not say what might happen. (Check the Master out before taking any training. *See* **What is a Reiki Master?**). If the initiating Master has not been initiated to attune and train others to use Reiki, then the person being initiated will not be channelling Reiki after the 'attunements'. This is one of the reasons that you need to be fully confident that your choice of initiating Master is what they claim to be.

Can we expect all Reiki Masters to be enlightened and well balanced people?

No. Reiki Masters are only human, treading their own paths, suffering from the human condition and its frailties. They have off days too. However, in joining with Reiki they have taken an important step towards their growth to enlightenment. Becoming a Master should not be undertaken lightly as it has responsibilities that go with it. Traditionally, the term 'Master' would have indicated that they had mastered *themselves* and had spent much time on their own personal development, as well as their chosen discipline. However, today it may only indicate that they have been attuned to the Third Degree of Reiki, and that they have the knowledge of how to pass initiations. They may have a way to go before becoming a Master in the traditional sense.

Does Reiki always feel hot when it is coming through?

No. Some treatments I have given have been very beneficial, yet the energy has been icy cold. However, it is far more common for the energy to be warm to scorching! I treated a friend throughout her pregnancy. Before becoming pregnant the Reiki would manifest as warmth, but once she was pregnant when treating her 'bump' it would immediately turn icy cold. Treatments returned to warm after the birth.

If you feel nothing, either when receiving or giving a treatment, does it mean the Reiki is not coming through?

No. Sometimes we are not sensitive to the sensation. Desensitisation can be caused by something as transitory as being tired or emotionally upset or in cases of illness when the body may have put up its defences in an attempt to cope with the illness. Continued contact with Reiki will bring about 'resensitisation'. Also those new to Reiki may need a time of adjustment to be able to perceive and recognise the energy sensations. Self-treatment helps here.

The Roots of Reiki

The energy of Reiki is as old as time. However, the system that is known as Reiki and also *The Usui System of Natural Healing* and *Usui Shiki Ryoho*, was brought into being by Dr Mikaomi Usui in the late 19th century.

There are two main branches of Reiki – one in the West, and one in Japan where Reiki originated. Both of these branches have many 'twigs' leading from them. Reiki was brought to the West in the late 1930s by Mrs Hawayo K. Takata and, along with it, her version of how it was founded by Dr Usui.

There are many versions of how Usui discovered Reiki, after years of studying the teachings of Buddha, and how it developed up to the present day. This is because of the way the history of Reiki has been passed down – through an oral tradition.

An oral tradition

The history in the West has been maintained by an oral tradition. The exact facts are considered less important than the thread that runs through the story and what it illustrates. As with any oral tradition, as each person tells it, and each time it is told, it changes subtly, almost unnoticeably – but the fundamentals are still there, and it carries with it an energy that goes beyond words. It is also more than the story and the teller – the experience also includes a listener who hears. But what do listeners hear? Each time they listen, they will *hear*

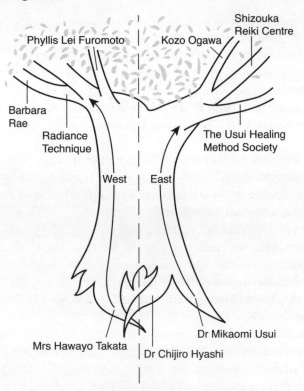

Some roots and branches of Reiki lineage

something different; they will hear what is most appropriate for them at that time, and if they go on to tell the story, they will tell it as they 'heard' it, and with the added influence of how they are at that moment.

If you have seen a film more than once, reread a book, listened to someone telling and retelling an incident, you will understand what I am trying to illustrate. There will be bits that you see/hear/read that you did not pick up previously, or in the case of the retelling of a happening were not told in the first place. You will also be affected by the *atmosphere* and *mood* of the source, and your reaction will also depend on your own mood at the time. Can you appreciate how the exact details can mutate and evolve?

Below is my version of this history as I heard it. Unfortunately this is not in audio form, but I am sure that the words, with some help from Reiki will be able to convey some of the energetics to you. The *hearing* I leave to you.

The origins of Reiki as told in the West
Dr Mikaomi Usui

In the latter part of the 19th century a man lived in Japan. His name was Dr Mikaomi Usui.

Dr Usui taught boys in a Christian School, where they studied the Bible. He was fascinated by the stories of Jesus and his healing abilities. One day his students asked him if he believed in the stories of the healing practices of Jesus. He said he did. They challenged him to explain and prove them. He found he couldn't and this set him thinking.

Eventually he left the school in order to search for some answers. He travelled all over, including to the USA, but he did not find the answers that he sought. What he did find was that all the healers that he studied healed through the laying on of hands. He returned to Japan and went to a Buddhist monastery. There, he meditated and studied, and became great friends with the head of the monastery. As he studied the sutras he found a part that caught his attention. He read and reread it many times, and finally, after several years he felt himself ready to receive the extra knowledge to make what he had already found complete.

He decided to go up a mountain by the monastery to fast and meditate. Before he left, he said to his friend, the holy man: 'If I don't return within twenty-one days, then send someone for my body.'

When he reached the top of the mountain he collected twenty-one stones. Each day he threw one away, so that he could keep track of the time passing. When he had only one left, and he had still not found the enlightenment he sought, he said to himself 'If something is going to happen, it must happen tonight.'

Just as dusk fell, he saw a bright light in the sky, and he noticed it was moving. All of a sudden he realised it was heading straight for him! His first instinct was to get quickly out of the way, but he thought: 'This might be just what I have been waiting for,' and so he just stood there and the light went straight for his head, and he fell into a trance.

We don't know all that happened in his trance, but it is said he saw wonderful coloured bubbles in which were golden symbols, and inside himself he knew the essence of these symbols.

When he came to, hours later, it was daylight. He jumped up, brushed himself down, cast away his last stone, and set off down the mountain. As you can imagine he was very excited and in his agitated state he managed to stub his toe painfully and caused it to bleed. He instinctively put his hand down to soothe it, and he found that in a few moments the pain had ceased and the bleeding had stopped.

'This is a miracle,' he thought, and carried on, down the mountain.

At the bottom of the mountain he saw a bench with a cloth over it – the sign of a roadside restaurant – so he went to it to take some sustenance. The owner was used to people calling to break their fasts with a light meal, so he was surprised when Dr Usui asked for rice and pickles. He advised him that he would be ill, and that he should have rice porridge only – this being the traditional meal to gently introduce food again. But no, Dr Usui would have none of it.

His meal was brought out by a woman who was in tears, and whose face was badly swollen on one side. He enquired what the matter was, and was told that she had a bad toothache. He put his hand to her face, and in minutes the pain had gone.

'A second miracle,' he thought. He then ate his breakfast and suffered no ill effects, which he mentioned to the owner.

'A third miracle,' he thought.

He went to see the head of the monastery. He told him what had happened, about the miracles and of the likelihood that he now had the ability to facilitate healing. The holy man warned him to be sure to treat the person as a whole, not just as a body, that is, to remember that each person is made up of a mind, a body and a spirit.

Dr Usui took time to think of what he would do next. He was excited, thinking of how he could help others with this newly-found skill. He decided to go to the slums and heal the poor, then he would help them to get jobs, which would enable them to live better lives. So off he went, and worked diligently for several years, healing and helping, feeling good about it all. But then he started to recognise the faces of those that he had healed previously, returning to him. He asked them what had went wrong. They told him that it was a lot easier not to have to work. He was disappointed, and stopped his healing work in the slums.

He then started to run through the streets during the daylight hours, bearing a lighted torch. People thought he was crazy, and called after him asking what he was up to. He replied, telling them to go to a certain place at a certain time if they wanted to know about the wonderful light that brightened the darkness. This is how he started to teach about Reiki.

Dr Chijiro Hyashi

One of Dr Usui's students was a Dr Chijiro Hyashi, who was a naval officer. He was weary of his lifestyle, and was looking to make changes, and do something different. Dr Usui seemed to have the answer for him. Dr Hyashi went on to open a clinic where he practised and had several people working for him.

Roots of the Western branch
Mrs Hawayo K. Takata

Mrs Hawayo K. Takata was a Japanese-American who lived in Hawaii, and a widow with two young children. She was seriously ill and was finding life difficult, feeling despondent, and even considered taking her own life but as she had children this was not an option. She spent much time praying, and felt that things would change. She decided to go to Japan to be near her family, and to look for a treatment there. It was obvious that she needed surgery, but she was so weak that she needed to build up her strength before she could consider it. When she had regained enough of her strength to be able to have surgery, and was waiting for the operation to be scheduled, she heard a voice saying that the surgery was not necessary. She ignored it but it spoke again. She pinched herself, and decided that if she heard it again she would do something about it. Sure enough, she heard it say 'Surgery is not necessary'. She asked her doctor if there was any other way, to which he replied 'yes', but that it would take time, and if she wanted to rush home, then it would have to be the operation. She decided to stay, and the doctor referred her to Dr Hyashi's clinic.

While she was being treated, she experienced a feeling of great heat coming from the practitioner's hands. She knew nothing about Reiki, so set about finding out what was causing it. She checked the table out, but found nothing. The next time it happened she grabbed the practioner's hands, who thought she wanted a handkerchief.

'No,' she said, 'where is the heat coming from?'

The practitioner thought this very amusing, but Dr Hyashi explained that although she looked Japanese, she was from America and did not understand about Reiki. She received Reiki for some months, and her health was healed.

Having been healed by this wonderful energy, she wanted to learn how to use it herself. However she was turned away.

At that time, no one outside of Japan had been trained to use it. She was adamant about learning, and promised to do anything, even to sell her home, if they would only teach her. Eventually they agreed to do so.

She went on to do a year's apprenticeship, learning and treating people. She was then initiated to the Second Degree and she returned home to Hawaii to practice. In time, she invited her Master Hyashi to Hawaii, and they spent six months working there together, teaching and practising. He then initiated her as a Master.

Within a year of Dr Hyashi returning to Japan, Mrs Takata had a dream, in which she saw him in a white kimono (this is the sign of death in Japan). She hastened back to Japan, and went to his house. She knocked on the door, and he came to the door and told her she was too early, and to come back at a particular time. She returned along with the other Masters that he had initiated. He told them many things. He said that Japan and the USA would come into a war together, and that he did not want to be part of it. He told Mrs Takata how she could keep her family out of the camps. He then said goodbye to them, ate his favourite food – a bowl of strawberries – and then laying down in his wife's arms made his transition.

Mrs Takata inherited his business, which she took care of and then returned home. All that Dr Hyashi predicted came to pass. Mrs Takata and her family remained safe and survived the war. She continued to practice long hours, every day of the week, doing housecalls. She committed her life to Reiki.

Mrs Takata made her transition in 1980 having initiated 22 Masters. She had been the head of the Western tradition.

Phyllis Lei Furomoto

After the death of the Mrs Takata some of the Masters moved away and set up their own lineages. One of these was Barbara Rae, and she called her lineage the Radiance Technique.

Practising Reiki

While those that stayed voted that Phyllis Lei Furomoto should take over from Mrs Takata and become their Spiritual Lineage Bearer and the Grand Master.

Ms Furomoto was Mrs Takata's granddaughter. So much of her life had been with Reiki, though much of it not consciously. She was the eldest grandchild and so got most of the responsibility for caring for her grandmother. She was initiated at an early age, and part of caring for Mrs Takata was to give her treatments in Reiki, it came into the same category as mundane household tasks! It was part of life. She was just instructed what to do, and she just did.

In her mid-twenties she was initiated to the Second Degree. She was taught how to use the distance healing and was then able to treat her grandmother when she was not actually with her. Mrs Takata always knew if she hadn't sent the treatment!

In time Mrs Takata started to take some time off, and went into semiretirement. But this was not what she really wanted, so she planned a trip. Her daughter was not happy with this, and felt that she should have a companion to travel with. Phyllis was volunteered. One day Mrs Takata asked her to sit, her feet on the floor and her hands above her head. Her grandmother initiated her as a Master and said 'Now you are ready to help me.'

They went on their trip and Ms Furomoto began to *learn* about Reiki for the first time, though she had been using it for ages. At this time only the Grand Master initiated Masters, while Masters where able to initiate to first and Second Degrees. When Ms Furomoto became the Grand Master she allowed other Masters to initiate new Masters. Now they are able to train and initiate all three Degrees, however most lineages recommend that new Masters work in their new Degree for some time to gain experience for themselves before initiating another Master.

The Eastern branch

In Japan, it would appear Reiki has just carried on, uninterested in and unaffected by the Western explosion of Reiki. Frank Arjava Petter has written a book that tells of his research so far, into the historical facts of the origins of Reiki. Here are the basics. For more detail read his book *Reiki Fire*, and then keep an eye out for the sequel which I am awaiting with eager anticipation. Mr Petter came to most of his information through a Mr Oishi, who had trained with one of Dr Usui's initiates.

Dr Mikaomi Usui

Reiki, though it was not called that, was part of a Buddhist offshoot of Qi Gong (a meditative movement revealing and cultivating the vital life force, inseparable from life itself), with an added Shontoist influence. Dr (non-medical) Mikaomi Usui rediscovered it towards the end of the 19th century and renamed it *"Rei-ki"*.

He was born on the 15th August 1862 in Yago village, situated in the Yamgata district of the Gifu prefecture in southern Japan. He married Sadako Suzuki and had two children. He died on the 9th March 1926 after his third stroke. He is buried at Saihoji temple, a mainstream Buddhist temple in the suburbs of Tokyo.

Dr Usui had run a business which had failed and left him with heavy debt. He felt he wanted something more in life than just material gain. He used to meditate by a waterfall on Mt. Kurama and it is said that one day he had a flash of insight. He went on to found *Usui Reiki Ryoho Gakkei*, *The Usui Healing Method Society*. He was its first president, and there have been five since. These were Mr Taketomi, Mr Watanabe, Mr Wanami, one whose name Mr Petter's contact could not remember, and the present one who is Ms Koyama.

Practising Reiki

Mr Kozo Ogawa and Mr Oishi

Dr Usui regularly taught workshops, and trained around 2000 students. There were many Reiki centres and clinics throughout Japan. The Reiki centre in Shizouka was run by a Mr Kozo Ogawa who had initially sold school uniforms. If he came across a sick child on his travels he would treat them with Reiki. He was skilled at knowing just how many treatments would be required to heal a person, and Dr Usui had recognised his healing expertise and elevated him to the highest rank within the Reiki organisation. Dr Usui and Mr Ogawa would give Reiki-charged crystal balls to their students. These could be placed against the patient's problem area. When the students were initiated they would receive a manual containing a description of Reiki, symptoms and guidelines for treatments. In those times the distance healing was called the 'photograph method', and as photos were rare, it would have been mostly the well off that would have benefited from this form of healing.

At Reiki meetings Mr Ogawa would recite the five Reiki principles out loud. Those who attended would have their healing abilities estimated by kneeling in the traditional manner with their hands folded in front of their chest, and Mr Ogawa would come along and touch their hands. Mr Oishi attended these meetings often and one day he was told that he had outstanding healing abilities. Mr Ogawa had no children and asked Mr Oishi to take over from him running the clinic in Shizouka City as he was now getting too old to carry on. Mr Oishi declined as he had heard that doing healing work would diminish his own life force. This is not so with Reiki.

By the 1940s there were about forty schools of Reiki spread throughout Japan with the system split into six Degrees. The content of these six Degrees is the same as those taught in the three Degrees today. They also used the same symbols that we use today.

The Reiki Principles

There are five Reiki principles. They were derived from some set by the Meiji Emperor of Japan (1818–1912). They are guidelines for gaining happiness in life. The brilliant thing about them is that in bringing yourself happiness by using them, you also bring benefits to all living things, including your planet, your nearest and dearest and your not so near and dear, to everyone and everything. Yes it really can reach that far. Anyone being initiated into Reiki should be willing to incorporate these principles into their lifestyles. They are in fact so obvious as life 'improvers' that I cannot see why anyone, whether of Reiki or not, would not follow them. There are many versions of them. Some have been customised by Masters, to make them more appropriate to the culture in which they are working, while others have been translated differently. Anyway I include various forms so that you will see the threads that run through them all.

They should be repeated frequently to re-enforce them in our lives. Contemplating on them will highlight different things at different times in life, and this can be quite revealing. They stand all people in good stead, and putting copies in places where you will glance them as you go about can help to remind us all, whether Reiki-ists or not of how to have a better way of life. Suggestions of where you might put them could include by the sink, on the fridge, by your mirror, on the dashboard of your car, in your purse or wallet, on your desk, in the bathroom, etc.

Here is a small selection of versions.

Versions of Reiki principles
Version one
1 Don't get angry today.
2 Don't worry today.
3 Be grateful today.
4 Work hard today (meditative practice).
5 Be kind to others today.

Frank Arjava Petter

Version two
1 Just for today do not anger.
2 Just for today do not worry.
3 Honour you parents, teachers and elders.
4 Earn your living honestly.
5 Show gratitude to every living thing.

Karyn Mitchell

Version three
1 Just for today I will let go of anger.
2 Just for today I will let go of worry.
3 Just for today I will give thanks for my many blessings.
4 Just for today I will do my work honestly.
5 Just for today I will be kind to my neighbour and every living thing.

William Lee Rand

Version four
1 Just for today, endeavour not to worry.
2 Just for today, endeavour not to anger.
3 Just for today, count your many blessings.
4 Just for today, work diligently and honestly, including on yourself.
5 Just for today honour all living things.

(This is the version I use) *Jennie Austin*

Working with the principles

One way of working with these principles, is to select one, and sit and contemplate it with specific reference to you and your life. Just sit quietly, and let the thoughts flow. If you have a problem doing this, then I offer you a few starters, but please do explore them for yourself, making them appropriate to you on a personal level. The following is just to get the cogs moving! I hope that even if you do not become initiated into Reiki, that you will still consider them as a good way to live. As with any new venture setting achievable goals makes it that much easier, so take it a day at a time to introduce any changes you choose to make.

Just for today endeavour not to worry

Worry is an energy stealer. It causes damage to the physical and mental self, and can contribute towards quite serious illness. Worrying about worrying can be a worry in itself. So don't get caught in that vicious circle. Be aware of the worry and try to let it go. If you are finding it impossible to let go, here are some questions that might help the process.

- What am I worried about?
- Why does this worry me?
- What is the worst that can happen?
- Am I just speculating on an event?
- Can I do anything about it?
- If 'yes' then do, if 'no' then you could try to do something alternative and positive with your time instead. Clearing the decks of your mind can often leave space for a new solution to pop in. Take a deep breath or two, and busy yourself – why not do some Reiki!

Just for today endeavour not to anger

Anger is another energy eater. Don't act with anger if you feel angry – it's a waste of precious energy in a negative manner. Anger is a natural mechanism, but there are some ways to counter it if you do feel your temper getting out of control:

- If you feel anger rising, take a deep breath, and ask what or who you are really angry at.
- If it is someone else, is it because the person does not hold the same view as you?
- Has someone done something differently to the way you would have done it?
- Has the person just made a mistake? No one is infallible.
- Put yourself in the place of others – experience how they might feel.
- Honour their views, allow them their frailties.
- You might also see if really it is yourself you are angry at. We can often see a reflection of ourselves in others. Explore your own anger.

Just for today count your many blessings

In our society we are always being told what we must have. It is a kind of brainwashing, trying to make us believe that everyone else has more than we do, and that the grass is greener on the other side of the fence!

- Take stock of the good things in your life. Try writing a list. Include not just those things of monetary value, but those things that are beyond gold, such as our families, friends, the roofs over our heads (however humble they might be), our health, drinking water, our freedom . . .
- Take a moment or two to imagine life without them.
- Another few moments considering others less fortunate than oneself can be very focusing.

Just for today work diligently and honestly, including upon yourself

Do an honest day's work. Be honest about how you earn your living. We only have to look around or watch the news to see that society now accepts a level of what I would class as dishonesty, and it costs each one of us dearly. Here are a few questions that you might like to consider.

- What would you do if someone overcharged you or you were not given enough change? How would you feel?
- What would you do if you were undercharged or given too much change? How would you feel?
- What would you do if you found a wallet containing money or an item?
- How would you feel if you lost your wallet or an item?
- How easy do you find it to tell a fib or a lie?
- How easy do you find it to withhold information and in so doing be misleading?
- How would you feel if someone took something that you had created, and profited from it without giving you anything?
- The feeling of achievement that can be experienced when a good day's work has been done is hard to better.

The older meaning of this principle meant that you should work to improve yourself and in so doing you would benefit both yourself and others around you. We cannot change others, yet by changing ourselves we can affect them. You probably know someone who is nice to be with, and being with them makes you feel good – see what I mean? We have to start somewhere and with ourselves is the only place we can start.

Just for today honour all living things
This includes our planet, our environment, all creatures, fellow humans – all colours and creeds and don't forget yourself too. We are all part of a whole. Whatever we do to one will eventually effect that whole and that includes ourselves. Honouring others' points of view, though it may not be the same as ours. Considering before we do something, to see if in gratifying our needs we are not causing detriment to someone

else. Knowing that we are all made by the Creator, and that each has an equal part to play in the bigger view, and without that part the picture would be incomplete.

- How do I think about me?
- Do I like me?
- What will the effect be if I speak or act in a particular way? Will it cause discomfort to another or harm them in any way? How will it affect me?
- What will the effect be if I don't say or act in this particular way?
- How can I live more in harmony and still care for myself?

Try these principles for twenty-one days (and beyond I hope). Go on, have a go. Life can change overnight, though it may not be easy to break the old habits.

(Twenty-one days is a recognised time, recommended to introduce you to any habit-breaking behaviour or regime of change.)

The Reiki precepts

1 The person seeking healing must have the real desire for change, the desire to be healed completely.
2 There should be an exchange for Reiki, whether it be money or and energetic one; this is to honour Reiki, and to accept true healing, while removing the conditions of obligation and control.

Receiving a Treatment with Reiki

I remember going for my first aromatherapy massage and feeling really apprehensive, as I did not know the *etiquette* or what was expected of me. I was shown behind a screen and told to get ready! 'Ready – how? Should I get undressed now? All off, or just a bit? And which bits should I leave? Should I stay standing, sit or lie down?'

Not ever having had a massage before, I was not at all sure and this put me into an even worse state of stress (the main reason for my visit). As I have mentioned before, Reiki is practised by a diverse selection of people with equally diverse ways of treating with it. Reiki is the only constant. Even the reactions to a treatment will vary, as of course there is diversity in the people who receive the treatments. However I hope that the following will act as a point of reference, and offer you some pieces of information that you may like to check out before being treated, and so get the maximum benefit from your treatment.

There are two basic ways of treating with Reiki. One is the hands-on method and the other is through distance healing (*see* **Distance Healing**). There are also two types of Reiki practitioner with whom you might get treatment. One is the professional Reiki practitioner, the other is someone who has been initiated to Reiki, but does not practice it as a profession, but on a more casual level. Some of the following will only apply to a visit to a practitioner, but much is also applicable to a more casual situation.

Hands-on method
Preparation

- For this method you will obviously be required to be present when the treatment is given.
- Allowing yourself time to arrive without rushing will help you to be more receptive to the Reiki, and if you don't have to start rushing about straight after, or go playing sport, it would give Reiki the space to work fully.
- Make sure you know exactly where you are going to have a treatment, to avoid any confusion.
- Forewarn the person who is going to treat you of any special requirements, e.g. that you have trouble climbing stairs, lying down, allergies or illnesses.
- The treatment can be administered with you sitting, lying or, in particular circumstances, standing (e.g. if a friend was treating a painful elbow, while you were waiting in a queue). Usually the treatment is given lying down, as this is more relaxing than if you are sitting up. Many Reiki-ists have treatment benches, while others treat on the floor, or even the dining table! For those in a wheelchair or in bed, treatments can still be carried out with no problems. For you the most important thing is that you are comfortable. Say if you are not.
- You do not need to remove clothes to receive Reiki. However, for your comfort, you will probably want to take off your overcoat and shoes, also loosen or remove any things that might cause restriction such as belts, ties, jewellery. Quartz watches should also be removed, as they emit tiny electromagnetic charges of energy, that can challenge your systems. Reiki will work around it, but you want to give yourself the best option. Some Reiki-ists like you to remove any crystals or gems as well.
- For your comfort it is advisable not to eat a heavy meal before, or just after a treatment. Because the body relaxes, and energy goes to carry out any detoxification, the food

will probably just lie in the digestive system. This can lead to a bloated feeling and sometimes slight nausea.

- It's a good idea to go to the loo before you start your treatment, so that you can relax fully.
- Eye glasses should also be removed as one of the positions for treatment involves covering the eyes. If you have contact lenses you may want to remove them as you will have your eyes shut, and you could well fall asleep.
- The Reiki-ist may want to take a case history, especially if you are attending for a specific reason. Some do not do this, especially if it is not a professional treatment. Although Reiki does not need to know what your problems are, it is helpful for practitioners to have some insights so that they can give you the full benefit of their skills.

During the treatment

- Once you start having your treatment, it is likely to be advantageous if you do not talk, unless it is necessary for your wellbeing. The Reiki-ist will not expect you to hold a conversation. However if you do need to talk, then the Reiki will carry on, despite you. If you don't talk, you are more likely to reach a deeper state of relaxation, hence removing tension and any resistance. It is easy to chatter while having a treatment with a friend but if you're not careful the experience of the actual treatment will pass almost unnoticed and you will have lost an integral part of the benefits. I have agreements with my friends, that we set time aside after or before the treatment to talk and have a cup of tea, but during the treatment we only talk if absolutely necessary.
- Close your eyes while being treated. Though this is not a 'must do' it will enable you to drift off and relax more easily. This is not a social event so you are not expected to be alert and communicative!
- During the treatment you may experience feelings of

warmth, heat, coolness, cold, tingling, pressure, a sensation of lightness or heaviness, your body temperature may rise or fall (if you feel cold, do ask for a blanket.) You may feel as though your body is rearranging and coming into line. You may jerk and twitch as tension leaves your muscles. You may drift into sleep, perchance to dream! You may even snore! That's OK, lots of people do – and tummies often rumble, not only the healee's! You may also experience sensations in places where you have had ailments in the past, or have them at present. This is just the Reiki working away. If you experience nothing else, you will probably feel relaxed and at peace.

- If you experience no sensations at all, don't think that nothing has happened. It will probably be just that you are not at that time sensitive to feeling this particular energy. Your sensitivity can vary from treatment to treatment, dependent on your condition and stress levels.

After treatment you *may* experience certain aftereffects

I don't want to pre-suggest that you will experience aftereffects but I would like to give you information that will set your mind at rest if you do. When I first experienced the symptoms of a detoxification, I became very concerned, not having been told that there was such a thing. Although on the face of it you may initially think that these are *side effects,* I would ask you to look on them positively and refer to them as *aftereffects.* The difference being that the term *side effects* is usually used when referring to the adverse reaction to a drug. I use the term *aftereffects* to describe a transitory happening, that is only a reaction to the treatment, that although not pleasant, is a means to an end – namely an improvement of condition. Most of these aftereffects are related to the detoxification process that can take place, as the body rids itself of toxins that hinder its efficient functioning and wellbeing. Others are signs that the body is healing itself and re-sensitising.

Reflex actions
You should be aware that your reflex actions may not be as fast as usual after a treatment, due to the levels of relaxation experienced with Reiki. So be mindful if driving or operating machinery or even just walking around town amongst traffic. Take time to bring yourself back to a fully aware state.

Sleepiness
You may experience a desire to rest/sleep, in which case if you can, it would be a good thing to do. This will enable the balancing, self healing and detoxification processes all to carry on unhindered.

Increased energy
You may feel energised, and have the desire to spring clean, run a marathon, climb a mountain – just don't overdo it.

Detoxification
The main detoxification symptoms include: needing to go to the loo more often, sometimes experiencing looser bowel movement and strong urine, nausea, headaches, runny nose (you may think you have a cold), increased salivation, increased perspiration (best not to suppress with antiperspirants), flatulence, spots (just cleanse regularly). Drinking plenty of plain water will help, also some gentle deep breathing – though don't do to much, just a few deep breaths every so often is fine. Please don't be put off by the above, most people don't experience any of them.

Change in menstrual cycle
Women may find that their periods change in character and rhythm. This is usually only temporary though they generally settle into a more balanced cycle.

Practising Reiki

Achieving a natural balance

If you are having regular treatments and are on medication, it would be wise to liaise with your doctor, in case you need to change the dosage. Sometimes, as the body reaches a state of better harmony it does not need so much help to maintain the status quo.

Again I must stress that these are beneficial reactions. They are a sign that the body is clearing and healing. If you have any concerns then contact your Reiki-ist.

Ways of Using Reiki

Reiki is useful in all areas of your life. It can be applied either in thought or by placing a Reiki-ist's hand on whatever is needing it; either themselves, another or even an inanimate object. In some cases it can be projected at something. Those initiated to the Second Degree can use Reiki irrespective of time or distance. Sounds too good to be true, I know, but it works. So here are just a few ideas of how it can benefit. The only limiting factor is the imagination.

Reiki in the home
Cooking
The good thing about Reiki is that you cannot put in too much or too little. It seems to be self-regulating! Tricky things like bread and pastry respond very well to it. It can be added as you work with your hands kneading or 'breadcrumbing', or just by placing your hands around the dough or pastry and giving it a treatment! Stirring Reiki into porridge or soup makes it just that bit more special.

Food and drink
Drinks and food can also be energised by placing the hands around the object and treating. This could be thought of as a kind of blessing. In this way the person who eats or drinks it will get an internal Reiki treatment! This can be very useful

Reiki-ing food and drink

when a quick pick-me-up is needed, and there isn't the time or space to do a treatment. It's also helpful for people who are ill. (Reiki the grapes when you go to visit someone in hospital.)

Feng Shui
The 'feeling' of the home can be enhanced with Reiki. If there has been discord, this can be neutralised. It is useful when practising Feng Shui.

Housework
Any tasks done with Reiki seem to be less of a drudge. It brings us more into tune with the job at hand.

Crystals in the home
Crystals are becoming more common in our homes and work-places, and they are more then inanimate objects. Harry Oldfield (The inventor of Electro-crystal Therapy) has photographed

energy forms in some of them. When I was visiting a crystal shop I noticed a dull and lifeless quartz cluster. I thought it probably just needed a gentle wash in mild soapy water. Feeling sorry for it, as it looked so sad, I purchased it and brought it home and gave it a wash. This didn't have any effect. So I placed it on a shelf that I passed a hundred times a day, so that I could send it a shot of Reiki every time I passed. Along with this I gave it daily treatments of a few minutes each, and gradually it began to sparkle. Now it is one of the crystals that visitors want to touch.

Gifts
Sending gifts and cards to people is a lovely tradition. Adding Reiki to them before giving makes them even more acceptable. It is like putting an invisible bow on it, and it won't crush in the post!

Bills
Paying bills! Add a little bit of Reiki when you pay your bills. Remember you are helping someone to earn their living.

Bathing
Reiki-ing the bath water is a good relaxer and revitaliser.

Minor health problems
First aid
It works well in first aid situations and with minor health problems. Helping to stem minor bleeding, calm panic, reduce or remove pain, take the sting and irritation out of insect bites, ease aching muscles and joints, strains and pulls, stiffness, headaches, skin problems, toothache, PMT, PMS and many more. It aids in recovery too, in instances such as tooth extraction. If given before the extraction it can dramatically reduce the loss of blood and the aftereffects.

Tantrums

Reiki is good at calming tantrums in children. Distance healing is very helpful here, because even if you are in the same room as the child, it is not always easy to do hands-on Reiki!

Stress

Reiki is great for reducing stress. Hardly anyone is immune from this terrible affliction. For many it is unwelcome, yet often it is a compulsory part of their lives. Reiki can help to reduce the adverse effects by supporting and calming the person, and feeding all the systems and strengthening them, so that they have less chance of any of them failing.

A complementary therapy

If it is necessary for anyone to have any treatment or medication Reiki will support it safely and without conflict, and in some cases, the requirement for medication can be reduced. This should only be attempted with the full knowledge and guidance of the prescribing doctor.

Negative emotion

It can help to calm emotional turmoil, and dispel negative thought patterns, such as anger, fear, hurt, jealousy, hatred, lack of self-confidence, guilt.

Gardening

In gardening it can be a boon. Plants seem to love it and respond by flourishing. I have treated many plants that looked as though they were done for, and they have gone on to bloom and grow and give much pleasure (*see* **Personal Insights**).

Pruning

When plants are pruned (I hate cutting plants back, but sometimes it is necessary), it can shock them, especially if you do it at the wrong time of year. Reiki-ing them by putting the hands around either the roots, if possible, or the foliage and flowers and treating them, can help them to overcome the trauma. A pre-snip treatment is also a good idea. If you have a number of plants that need treatment, then the water can be Reiki-ed before it is poured on them. Plants don't need to be in stress to benefit, healthy ones enjoy it too, and usually re-pay by becoming even more happy and abundant.

Sprouting seeds

If you are into sprouting seeds, such as alfalfa, mung beans and mustard and cress, you can cut the production time down quite considerably, and increase their vitality, which is passed on to the eater. I usually suggest that the newly-initiated try this, as it is easy to see the effect of Reiki if you also grow a control batch.

Just by holding a packet of seeds between the hands, and treating for five minutes, or until the flow stops, they will receive a shot of vital life force, which will give them a good start. This can be shown when sprouting seeds such as alfalfa and mung beans. Many of my past initiates have tested their Reiki ability by planting two lots, one as a control, and one for treating with Reiki. In just a few days there is a noticeable difference between them. However beware of passive Reiki. One person reported that both his trays grew like mad! They need to be kept in the same environment but far enough apart, so that when the Reiki tray is being treated the control one does not also get a treatment.

House plants

Treating a house plant, trays of bedding plants and shrubs from the nurseries before planting is simple. Quite often plants have had a rough ride, with shocks in temperature as well as jolts and bangs, on their journey from seed or cutting to their final growing place. Just by placing the hands around the pot with their roots in, or around their foliage, if they have any, they are able to take in the Reiki. This helps them to re-cover and grow healthy and happy. More than one plant can be treated at a time by holding the hands above a small group of plants.

Watering

A simpler way of getting Reiki to more than one plant is to Reiki the water before watering or misting them. This is easy to do too. Just put the hands around the water container, en-abling the Reiki to flow, and bingo! Reiki-charged water. This is particularly useful for newly-planted shrubs, seeds or bed-ding plants in the garden. One person that I had initiated said that she had pruned her roses back a bit late, and that she hoped the Reiki would help them recover, but it was taking

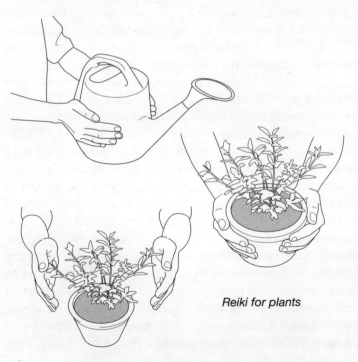

Reiki for plants

her all evening giving each one a five-minute treatment. Once she started watering them with Reiki-water the whole operation only took ten minutes or so. It worked very well.

Vegetables

When I say plants and seeds, I include the vegetable kingdom as well. If you have a large vegetable patch, you will be adding up the number of watering cans that you use each evening, and multiplying this by five minutes etc. It's OK. Remember you are only limited by your imagination. Here are a couple of suggestions to cut the time involved. Reiki the water butt. Reiki some quartz crystals by holding them in your hand, when you are not doing anything else. I usually have a couple in my pocket, which I can charge as I wait in a queue, or sit talking to someone. I do it automatically now, without thinking. They can then be placed in the water for the plants for five minutes or more, while other tasks are being done.

If you are into hugging trees, then adding Reiki to the hug makes it even more special.

Treating animals with Reiki

Animals love Reiki, and will often gravitate to where a treatment is being carried out. They respond well, and often for less serious problems a visit to the vet or doctor, or the need for use of over the counter medicines can be avoided.

Animals are so sensitive that they are often able to help us to do what is best for them. Although a modified version of the human treatment sequence can be attempted, they very often position themselves under the hands so that the Reiki goes where it feels best for them. Some initiates have noticed that their pets look at them questioningly when they first return after being trained, but that once they have got used to the new version 'mum' or 'dad' they are eager to get their dosage of Reiki on a regular basis.

I have found that if an animal has a part of it that is ailing, it

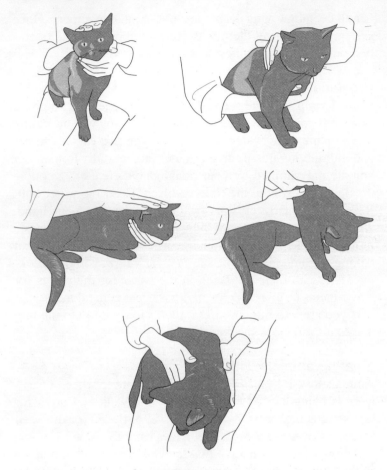

Reiki on a cat

will sometimes prefer that the Reiki is not put straight onto it. I suggest that this might be because as the balancing required to bring about the healing starts, it creates sensations that the animal does not recognise, and in some cases causes temporary discomfort and so it moves away. Because the Reiki moves freely around the body, finding the areas of most need, it doesn't matter where the Reiki is applied. Animals also help

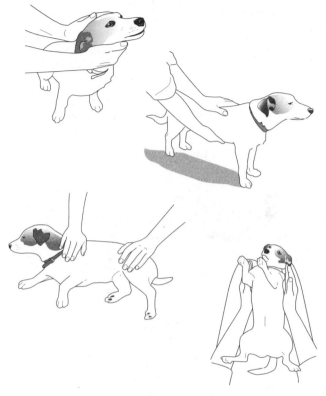

Reiki on a dog

in deciding when it is time to move from one position to another, and in choosing where the next position is.

Never force treatment on an animal

A treatment can be as casual as a cuddle. For instance just placing your hands on a cat as it nestles on the lap, or resting a hand on a dog's head as it sits beside you, can be all that is required. **Never** force an animal to have Reiki. If it moves away from your offer, accept this. Animals have their rights too.

Behavioural problems

Reiki can help with all sorts of problems, not just those with physical manifestations. It can also be helpful when there are character or behavioural problems.

Distance healing

Distance healing is useful with animals as well. Not all creatures are touchable. These include farm animals and wildlife. It is very simple to send distance healing to them. All we need is the desire to help them, the Second-Degree initiation and a way of identifying them for ourselves. If you are wanting to help a whole herd of deer for instance, then you could identify them by location, e.g. 'Please send Reiki to all the deer in Dell Wood'. If it is a cow in a field, you can identify it by a marking, or even by the ailment, e.g. 'Please send Reiki to the cow in the meadow who has a poorly leg' or 'the cow with the white spots on her left side'. The important thing is your intent; the fact that you know who you mean inside yourself. To ensure that the animal has a choice, something like the following should be added: 'If she chooses to receive the Reiki and for the good of all concerned.'

For those who have a pet that pines when they are away, hands-on healing helps to prepare them for the separation, and distance healing can help to maintain that special bond that is formed between a pet and its owner while offering comfort and an invisible connection. Reiki for the owner is also helpful, as I think we probably suffer as much as our pets!

Reiki at work
Stress reduction

Stress and its effects are now being acknowledged by most employers, as are the benefits of Reiki as a stress reducer by some of them.

Illness
Reiki can help to prevent many hours of absenteeism. Where someone might have stayed home, or not be able to complete the day with, for instance, a migraine, PMS, a bad back or even a hangover. Reiki can help them by assisting in the alleviation of symptoms, while helping the person back to a more healthy state. It can also increase their vitality levels.

Equipment
Machinery that is playing up, quite often responds favourably to a bit of Reiki. I know this sounds mad. I have included some instances in **Personal Insights**.

Good ideas
Inspiration can be invoked with Reiki. Very important if you are doing a presentation, writing a report, have an important meeting, doing an exam, or just having to keep your end up. Those who are initiated into Reiki often find their intuition increases. This has to be helpful in any situation.

Surroundings
Rooms can be made to feel *good* so improving the general atmosphere and ambience. Happy workers make for increased productivity and less absenteeism.

Plants in workplaces often suffer from neglect and adverse conditions – they really appreciate a bit of Reiki.

Documents
Reiki-ing proposals and contracts gives them a favourable air.

How to use Reiki in the workplace
Because Reiki is so versatile and adaptable it does not need any particular setting for a treatment to be given and for it to be of benefit.

I teach in the local college, and sometimes the students in

my class are unwell. Not bad enough to not come in, but unwell enough to hamper their learning. Ailments such as headaches, PMS, inflamed eyes, cramp, upset tummies, hangovers and all sorts. The courses in which they are participating are fairly intense, and so it is important that they are able to keep up with their learning. I quite often ask the student to sit with me, and I just put my hands on her, and give her a Reiki treatment while I am teaching the class. This does not in any way interfere with the teaching side of my role, as once I have started the flow, I usually am not paying any attention to the student having the treatment. I just keep on tutoring as normal, including waving my hands about and writing on the board, and Reiki does the rest. Despite this seemingly unsatisfactory Reiki treatment, the students benefit and are usually able to continue with their learning.

The shortest treatment I ever gave was two minutes. I was giving therapeutic treatments in a hotel, and one of the resident hairdressers popped in for a moan. She was obviously under the weather with a heavy cold, verging on 'flu. Her boss would not let her go home as she had two more clients to do, and the salon was fully booked. My colleague (also a Reikiist) and I shot each other a look, enquired how much time she had, and invited her to lie on the bench. We stood one at the head and one at the feet. We invited Reiki to join us, and POW! Two minutes later this lass got up, her nose clear, the aches in her limbs and head relieved, and appearing to have been revitalised. She dashed off to back to work. The next morning we were greeted by a chirpy smiling person with not a sign of the ailments of the day before.

The following is part of an article that Dorothy Berry-Lound wrote for the *Reiki Connections* newsletter.

From Dorothy Berry-Lound in Reiki Connections
I am the managing director of an extremely busy organisation researching trends in employment and training. We work to

extremely tight deadlines and the atmosphere can, at times, become quite fraught. Once I had come to terms with 'living' Reiki, as opposed to giving it allocated times in my schedule, I found I automatically began to apply it to workplace situations. The effects have been quite startling.

On a simple level, I regularly Reiki telephone calls or the offices themselves, often as part of space clearing which I do after any particularly hassled period. I make a particular effort to Reiki offices prior to meetings, sometimes applying a 'time capsule' principle to make the most of train journeys, setting up a release of Reiki for the beginning of a difficult meeting perhaps, or to allow for arriving slightly late at a meeting. I also Reiki beverages, buffet lunches, papers, pencils – you name it, it does not escape.

I hasten to add that none of this is done in any ostentatious way. I have become mistress of the sweeping nonchalant hand that covers a multitude of sins, so meeting attendees and staff are not aware I am doing it. Where someone is struggling in a difficult situation, I find I automatically send them Reiki with the balance symbols to help them formulate their ideas or put forward their views. Certainly, the meetings go much more smoothly with Reiki and people seem to leave feeling good about the experience.

I have found that more direct applications of Reiki with office staff also bears fruit. The Reiki, almost applied as first-aid really, has proved invaluable in dealing with the following few examples of the range of things that have cropped up:

- Relieving sinusitis blockages during the hay fever season. (Have you ever noticed how many people around you suffer from hay fever – once they realise Reiki can help, they come out of the woodwork.)
- Stress-related headaches.
- Aching wrists and hands due to computer keyboarding.
- Tired eyes (again from using the computer).

- Stress-induced panic (if you can get them to sit still long enough).
- Top-up treatments for sprained ankles etc (from the step class that half the office go to).
- Paper cuts and scalds.
- Period pains.
- General emotional upset.

Now you may be thinking where does the work get done if all this Reiki takes place.

I have developed a variation of the seated Reiki application that takes between ten to fifteen minutes (depending on the severity of the injury or problem, the most I ever do is 25 minutes). The individual participates fully – the office environment does not allow for silent treatment! I usually use my own office, light a joss stick (more for me than for them!), and put on some whale song or something similar as I have found the trick is to get them to relax as quickly as possible. Usually I get them to deep breathe with me to get the relaxation process underway and then the Reiki does the rest. Payment usually consists of a hug, some camomile tea and, frankly, increased productivity. On several occasions Reiki has been able to prevent the onset of migraines, enabling a member of staff to remain at work rather than taking the usual three days off sick.

In emergencies I have applied Reiki in situ rather than go through the ceremony of retreating to my room. I have been greeted on completion by other members of staff with big grins talking about having benefited from 'passive Reiki'.

So if you have never done so, I recommend Reiki for the workplace – it works.

Reiki in hospitals and hospices

Reiki can be marvellous here for both the patients, the staff and family carers.

Staff

The staff need to be happy, well motivated and fit to enable them to carry out the demanding work of caring for the sick and dying. They work in an atmosphere not just of healing but also of sickness and death, and the energies that go with these can have quite an adverse effect on those who are constantly surrounded by them. As Reiki is so versatile, it can be called upon in most circumstances. It can be used without any preparation or ceremony, for instance while walking between tasks, just placing a hand on the self can give an infusion of energy and wellbeing. Longer boosts could be given while taking a break, taking a phone call or writing up reports.

Visitors

Reiki is helpful for the family and friends that spend so much time and energy supporting the sick person. This can be tiring and time consuming. It can help to support them as well as giving them another tool to help the patient.

Pain-relief

Reiki can reduce pain and symptoms and so can reduce the need for painkillers and other drugs. It can give a transfusion of energy. Reiki does not need to be given formally, a well-placed hand can enable the flow, and it will then travel to where it is most needed, whether it is done for the patient or the carer.

For those who are dying, a reduction in drugs can enable them to make their transition consciously, rather than in a haze, not knowing whether they have gone or not, or whether the person in white is an angel or a nurse. Reiki is an effective pain killer and helps bring relief from many symptoms. I believe it also provides a bridge between this plane of existence and the next, and can be of help to the dying as they go along their way. It brings comfort to those who are left.

Practising Reiki

Food

Food can be Reiki-ed. This is a way of introducing Reiki for the benefit of the people who eat it, be they carers or patients.

Plants

The plants and flowers can be treated to help them stay lively in what is usually a hot and dry atmosphere.

Reiki with other healing modalities

Reiki should be valued in its own right as a therapy, but it can also complement other treatments without hindering them. I have personally used it with the following ones:

Aromatherapy

I have used it to vitalise the oils, so that they could carry the Reiki into the body, this is especially helpful when treatment methods other than massage or hands-on are used (e.g. inhalation, baths, compresses). When using massage, Reiki often comes through automatically, transforming not just the actual treatment session but the results as well.

Reflexology

Reiki frequently flows during a treatment. It doesn't have to be fed in at the ailing part, it can travel through the body and still reach the place that needs it most, so just touching the feet (or hands) can allow Reiki to work its wonders. I also think that it uses the reflex system, as I have noticed the intensity vary according to the reflex I am on, and the condition of the corresponding body part. (Reflexology is a treatment given through the feet, or sometimes the hands. The whole body and its organs are mapped onto the feet/hands, thus enabling specific parts to be assessed and treated without direct contact with the body part.)

Bach flower remedies

I also use the Bach flower remedies. They work well together, especially if the person is unable to come for frequent treatments. The Reiki can loosen up emotions, and the Bach flower remedies can help the person deal with them. Reiki can also help as the Bach flower remedies peel the layers of emotions away, by introducing one of the most important elements in healing work, that is, providing some touch, some hands-on comfort. Distance Reiki is also good in these situations although of course it doesn't have quite the same touch factor. Having said that, I have many reports from people who have received distance healing saying that they have 'felt' the treatment going on.

Medicines

Any medicine, whether alternative or orthodox can be Reiki-ed. It will give people taking it a bit of Reiki every time they take a dose, thus helping to counteract any adverse side effects.

Any treatments given usually show benefits more quickly. As you are helping the body to heal itself, there is less for the other treatment to do.

If there are any drugs involved, Reiki helps the systems to cope with any toxins or symptoms of side effects.

Reiki and self-development, awareness and care

Reiki is so good at this. Sometimes it is an introduction to your own personal path, and once on the way it produces opportunities for you, challenges that stretch you just a bit to help you grow, but never more than you can deal with, and of course it supports and aids in a multitude of ways.

Addiction

It can help you to give up addictions – in fact many people find that they really go off something that they had constantly yearned for previously. (e.g. cigarettes, alcohol, drugs, animal products, some lifestyles.) Sometimes it takes a while, but it happens, much to many people's surprise. Having a true desire to succeed speeds the process up.

Meditation

Reiki in meditation is wonderful. A self-treatment becomes a meditation in itself. Often reaching bliss point. It helps to centre and quiet the mind. If doing a guided meditation it concentrates the focus, and the pictures are more distinct. Use of the Sacred Symbols can add an extra dimension and be very revealing.

Development of the senses

Intuition develops almost automatically. Life seems to just flow more easily. Perception and awareness of the world around you becomes stronger. The senses can become more acute.

Relationships

Reiki can help with relationships. It cannot be used to entrap someone, to make them fall for you, but Reiki can make you a more pleasing person to be with. One person reported back that since her initiation people were smiling at her and talking to her, when before she could have walked in and out of a room and no one would have noticed. Sometimes it is appropriate that a relationship dissolves, and in cases such as this it can help to make the end more acceptable and less painful.

Fears

For those who have fears, it can bring comfort and confidence, along with a general feeling of wellbeing often helping us to see that our fears have no real foundations, and if they do, it can give us the strength to face them. It takes the darkness out of the night.

Inanimate things

You may find this hard to believe but Reiki also works on inanimate and mechanical things.

One night I was printing some urgent work off my word processor, only to find that the printer was playing up. I shut it all down to see if a rest would help. On powering it up again, the fault was still there. I left it overnight, planning a visit to the menders and a bit concerned as to how I was going to get the work printed out. I tried again, and still it was not working. I went off, to make plans to go into town. Then it occurred to me to try Reiki. I went to the office, and gave it some Reiki. I turned it on, and wow! It worked perfectly, and it is still working well months later.

Reiki makes opening jars, etc. easier. The manufacturers seem to be making it harder and harder to get into their products

Try Reiki-ing traffic lights when you're in a hurry. Think green! Reiki-ing journeys is also a good thing to do. Reiki-ists have reported back that after doing so journeys seem to have gone more smoothly than could have been expected.

Further on in this book there is a section called **Personal Insights**. *This contains lots of real-life instances of when Reiki has been used.*

Stress and Reiki

Stress comes in many guises. We all need a bit of positive stress to give us the incentive to do things and to keep going. But there is the sort of stress that can cause overload and then it is detrimental to our wellbeing. This is the stress that puts undue strain on our systems, and which can eventually result in the breakdown of the perfectly designed mechanism that keeps us balanced, vital and experiencing good health and happiness. Some people seem to thrive on stress and the challenges that it can bring, but this can become addictive and in the long term is virtually suicidal. It is like driving a car flat out all the time without getting it serviced.

Some stress is self-inflicted while some is imposed on us and is beyond our control. In either case we have a choice of allowing it to affect us unchallenged or we can take precautions by fortifying ourselves and counteracting the adverse effects.

How does stress affect us?

At the mildest end of the scale it can just rob us of our vitality, but at the serious end it can bring on major illness and premature death.

It starts by getting our bodies to produce chemicals which were designed to give us the ability to either fight or run when challenged (the fight or flight mechanism.) As we mostly don't do either nowadays, they lodge in our tissues and immediately start hampering us. Stress also makes muscles tense which restricts the circulation of blood and lymph which feed our systems and take away the waste, including the stress-produced chemicals, thus keeping us in prime condition. Because of the hampered circulation, all the systems are put under more stress as they are having to function without proper fuel and with a backlog of waste – creating more stress for the body, and more stress chemicals and so on!

As far as symptoms are concerned, these come in many forms. They include headaches, insomnia, indigestion and malabsorption of nutrients, poor elimination of waste, upset tummies, poor memory function, poor concentration, irrational and illogical thoughts, addictions, agitation, panic attacks, sweating and temperature swings, shaking, aches, pains, skin problems, poor performance and lack of ability to cope, frigidity and impotence, high blood pressure, illness that is minor, serious and terminal.

What causes stress?

Some causes are out of our control, such as the air we breath, the water we drink, our atmosphere – which is filled with different waves e.g. microwaves, radar, radio, TV, mobile phones etc – frequencies, sound (not always heard), pollutants, they all put our systems under a strain. There are many stress inducers that are controllable or self-inflicted, however unconsciously or ignorantly taken on. These include our lifestyles, poor diet (not all that looks healthy is), addictions (including nicotine, caffeine, chocolate, alcohol, drugs, some medication), over- or under-exercise, negative thoughts and the influence of others over us. But all is not lost, we can counteract the effects, even if we can't control the source of the stress.

Guidelines for coping with stress

First of all, identify the source of your stress. If you can do something about it then do, today not tomorrow! If you can't then the best you can do is support yourself in dealing with the effects and maintaining a high level of condition to be able to deal with the stress as it comes to you.

Active

- Take exercise (check first with your doctor if you are in their care). It doesn't have to be a five-mile run or a game of squash, just a brisk walk every day or you could put on a cheery piece of music that you like, with a good beat and dance – the twist is excellent! Just move with joy, wave your arms around, move your feet, bend and twist, loosen up you muscles, get the circulation going. This will have the effect of ridding you of the accumulated waste and you will feel brighter too, and more vital. Even if you thought you had no energy to start with. Only do as much as you feel good with, overdoing it will only make matters worse.
- Drink plenty of water – bottled, filtered or boiled if your tap water tastes awful. Remember to Reiki the water before drinking it. You can Reiki a bottle-full at a time, or Reiki it as you hold it as you are sipping it.
- Breathe properly – every so often check on how you are breathing. Take a few deep breaths, fill your lungs from your tummy up, be careful not to overdo it. Three or four breaths several times a day will help. Increase this as your lungs and body get used to all that lovely oxygen. Eventually you will start breathing more efficiently.
- One place that stress often creates tension is in the shoulders and neck. This inhibits the flow of blood around the brain, quite apart from being uncomfortable. Remembering to breathe, move your head and neck around, then scrunch your shoulders up to your ears, taking a deep breath in and holding for a moment, then let your shoulders drop as you let your breath go in a big puff. Repeat several times. Hold Reiki-ing hands over the tense areas will help to relax and clear.

Semi-active
- Yoga, T'ai Chi or something similar. Gentle movement without strain.
- Reiki self-treatments done regularly.

Passive
- Taking exercise is important and, in addition, there are some lovely passive ways of helping yourself as well. Top of the list has to be Reiki – with someone else *doing it*. With Reiki you do not need to be specific about what you are treating and so Reiki will help to address any problems that have manifested or are on their way. Reiki distance healing is also a great aid here too, as so often, when stress is biting the hardest, there is little free time and the last thing you can fit in is a treatment for yourself.
- Taking some nutritional advice about diet can also help.

Step away from stress
If stress is biting, then Reiki is the thing. If you can step out of the situation for just a few moments to do a partial self-treatment, it is remarkable how everything looks different when you go back into the fray, and of course the batteries have been charged. Even if you can't step out, Reiki can still help. By putting a hand on the solar plexus stress levels can be brought down. Reiki-ing any drink or food that you ingest is another easy way to getting some Reiki help. Using the mental/emotional symbol to bring clarity (Second Degree), and even sending Reiki to whatever is causing the stress.

We cannot afford to ignore stress – it is a killer. We need to be aware and take action. It is unlikely to go away. Reiki is one of the most versatile, efficient and cost-effective ways of dealing with stress.

Reiki Training

Reiki is most often taught in three Degrees, though *The Radiance Technique* founded by Barbara Rae, uses seven Degrees. Some Masters offer extra levels, but the number of actual Degrees is still the same.

These Degrees must be done in order, each building on the previous stage. However, each one is complete in itself and so you do not have to complete all three Degrees. Many people do only the first, some go on to do the Second, while less feel the call to the Third. There are probably as many ways of presenting Reiki as there are Masters. Some add non-Reiki subjects, while others pare it down to the bare bones. The following is how I pass Reiki on at this present time:

The First Degree

This is the starting point of Reiki training. It is the Degree that I encourage my patients to do, so that they can take over their treatment completely or if they wish to continue coming to me, to supplement the treatments I provide. Daily self-treatments work wonders. This Degree introduces the student to the basics of Reiki. It enables them to work on themselves and others in a hands-on way. This is what the training includes:

- Four attunements – the passing of energy from the initiating Master to the student to balance and fine-tune them to enable them to channel Reiki themselves.
- The history of Reiki and information on the lineages.

- The five principles of Reiki.
- The two precepts of treating with Reiki.
- What Reiki is and how it works.
- Reiki's limitations and contra-indications.
- Suggestions on how Reiki can be used.
- Explanation and instruction on hand positions for treatments.
- Instruction on doing self-treatments, the benefits and how important they are.
- Instruction on treating others. (Sitting, lying, informal, specific problems)
- Information on possible reactions to Reiki.
- Guidance on healee care and comfort.
- Guidance on Reiki-ist care and comfort when giving treatments,
- Some thoughts on paths of self-development.
- Lots of practice, including giving and receiving treatments, so that new Reiki-ists go away confident that they can use Reiki.
- Time for questions and answers, discussion and voluntary sharing of any personal experiences relating to the Reiki.

At the end of the first month after the training, they are asked to present some reports on their use of Reiki, (e.g. treatments that they have done on others, situations, experiences). This is a check that Reiki-ists have understood, and are happily using their new skills, and that encourages them to keep on using Reiki when they leave the environment of the class, and get back into the outside world. They are also asked to keep a personal journal during that month (and hopefully beyond). This will enable them to chart the changes which are often only apparent when viewing with hindsight. I ask that they present a summary of this along with their reports. The homework bit sounds daunting to some, but guidance is given on the presentation and content. The more pronounced effects resulting from the initiation are experienced during the first month, and it is good to be able to experience these to the full. There is something called the 'twenty-one-day clearance period' straight after each level. This is when the bodies adjust to the new energetic matrix. It can be a very exciting time, with challenges that can be met easily, positive changes for the long term, and moments of exploration and of wonderment. However some go through this stage without much perceived change. This is where the journal helps, it focuses your attention on even the smallest detail. This was my experience, and it is only in looking back that I can see how much happened. But that is another story!

- On receipt of the reports and journal Reiki-ists are sent their certificate confirming their initiation.
- Post-initiation support is available for life.

I teach the First Degree over two days (i.e. four sessions) or the equivalent. Handouts are supplied, and also lunch if the course is held at my centre.

The Second Degree

This Degree is for those who have already completed their First Degree. Usually a period of at least three months should have elapsed since then. This enables the person to have experienced the First Degree's character and have assimilated the new energetics, balance and ability, in preparation for this Degree (hopefully he or she will have gained some experience as well). They should have space and the ability to take on board more information and advanced techniques. The Second Degree is often referred to as the practitioner level. Some do go into practice as a Reiki practitioner, though to be a professional more training is advisable. This training only teaches the skills of a more advanced form of Reiki. For those who wish to continue using it on family and friends it will offer them more tools to work with.

The content of the training is:
- One attunement: this enables the Reiki-ist to use an upgraded form of Reiki, including the Sacred Symbols.
- The Sacred Symbols are taught with their uses. It is expected that the student is prepared not to share these with anyone else, but to accept that they are sacred and should be kept for use by only those who have been initiated to do so. The student should have memorised these symbols before leaving the training. There is more information on these symbols in the chapter on Sacred Symbols.
- Lots of practice of using these symbols. Treatments are given and received.
- Some information on setting up and running a Reiki practice. (Further training on being a practitioner can be undertaken at another time if required).
- Time for questions and answers, discussion and voluntary sharing of Reiki experiences.
- The new Second-Degree Reiki-ist is asked to keep a journal following the initiation and to send me a summary of it and a record of their Reiki activities at the end of the month. Another twenty-one-day clearance period is experienced.

I teach the Second Degree over two days (i.e. four sessions) or the equivalent. Handouts are provided, and also lunch if the course is held at my centre.

The Third Degree – Master, Teacher
This Degree is for those who have completed both the First and Second Degrees and have been actively using Reiki. Prospective candidates are asked to apply in writing stating why they want to do this Degree, and what experience they have had. This is as much for them to clarify their motives as much as for me to have a starting point.

The time lapse should be at least six months after their Second Degree and two to three years between their First and

Third. The timing will vary depending on candidates and how diligent they have been with their Reiki working. Sometimes some extra work is required before commencement of the training.

This training is in the form of an apprenticeship. It takes around a year during which we meet and keep in contact regularly. Distance has not been a problem.

The candidates make the commitment and then continue to nurture their self-development in a manner of their choice, in liaison with me.

- They attend and observe my training workshops of both the First and Second Degrees, plan their own and produce their own handouts. This is to give them a point to start from in designing their own presentation.
- I attend and observe their workshops and teaching of both Degrees and offer feedback. This is not intended to turn them into clones of me, but to ensure that they are covering all necessary elements, and to identify any problem areas. It is also a comfort to have someone standing by until full confidence is gained.
- Each person's Master training is formulated for them personally, dependent on their abilities and requirements. For instance, some need help in developing teaching skills, while others already have this ability, and others may seek assistance in formulating their courses etc.
- The length of training allows the prospective Master/ Teacher to develop their skills and grow in themselves so that by the time they finish they will be responsible and able in their Mastership.
- Throughout the apprenticeship they keep a journal, read, continue with their self-development and of course work with Reiki. Summaries of their journal, book reviews and reports on their progress and experiences are sent to me monthly.

- One attunement is given.
- The Master symbol is learned. As with the Second-Degree Sacred Symbols this is not to be shared with others.
- Attunement procedures are taught and practised.
- Lots of contact is kept in between allowing freedom of growth within an atmosphere of support and suggestive guidance and sharing. This is not a situation of domination, but one of travelling alongside.

About the Sacred Symbols of Reiki

These symbols were shown to Dr Usui, the founder of Reiki, on the last day of a twenty-one-day fast and retreat up a mountain. He had studied for many years and worked on himself, and he undertook this retreat in order to be shown the information that would make whole this phenomenal system of natural healing.

There are four Reiki Symbols

Three symbols are given to those being initiated to the Second Degree.

The fourth is given in the Third Degree to Masters when they are initiated.

The symbols are given on the understanding that they are for the initiates' eyes only, and that they are not to be shared.

There are different versions of the symbols. There are a couple of possible explanations for this. It is said that in the West Mrs Takata gave each Master whom she initiated slightly different forms of them, specific to that particular Master's vibrations. Another explanation is that because no hard copy was given, they were passed on by word of mouth only, and variations may have been manifested from each person's perception and memory. In the same way that our writing differs from person to person, so would each person's interpretation. Over time, with nothing to refer back to, this possibly led to slightly different forms.

It is important that the initiates use the symbols that they are given by their Master, as these will be the ones that they have been attuned to use, and certainly no conscious action should be made to customise them.

The Sacred Symbols

The Sacred Symbols have not only form but also sound (i.e. a name). They have a common name, which can be used in conversation. The sound as well as the form has specific uses, and should only be spoken when being activated. It can be said internally rather than out loud if, for instance, it is being used during a treatment on, or in the company of, uninitiated persons.

In the following I will use the common names, as this book will be available to all.

If you are initiated to the Second or Third Degrees your Master will have given you your symbols, and told you *how* to use them. Here follows a few ideas on instances *when* they can be used.

The three Sacred Symbols given to the Second-Degree initiate

The power symbol
The first symbol is known as the power symbol. This is not power as in power over someone, but power as in voltage, octane, horsepower. This symbol enables the Reiki-ist to access a stronger, more focused version of the Reiki. It is not the stronger energy itself, but it is the key that opens the way for it to flow.

- This can be used when starting a treatment in preparation of the self to treat, and also to call the Reiki down.
- It can be used during a treatment, when extra focus or zap is needed, e.g. on an area that is depleted of energy or in need of special care.
- It can be used to energise anything that could benefit from

the energy, such as a plant, seedlings to encourage strong growth, a glass of water for someone to drink (an internal Reiki quickie and booster), pre-made sandwiches, to charge a crystal for placing against an ailing part, a gift, card or letter – it carries the universal love with it.

- Also medicines, massage oils, earth and water for plants can all be charged.
- It can be used for protection, for instance if you are in a hostile environment, or with people who *take* from you, or when you are undergoing an onslaught of emotional flack. It can help to protect property, and be used anywhere else that protection is needed.
- It is helpful in clearing, strengthening and for the sealing of the energetic body, i.e. the aura and chakras.
- It can be a focus for meditation.
- If you have any *dark* or *cold* corners in for instance your home, office or garden, it can help to lighten and warm them.
- If you are cold it can help to warm you.
- If you are feeling in need of an energy boost it can help.

The mental/emotional symbol

The second symbol is known as the mental/emotional symbol.

- This is a wonderful symbol that can be used to help balance the mental and emotional elements. This in turn helps to bring balance (as opposed to dis-ease) into the physical.
- It can be used to break the hold of negative thoughts and help to transform them.
- It can bring peace and clarity to the thoughts, and is helpful in memory lapses, you know when you have it on the tip of your tongue but . . . !
- It helps to soothe mental turbulence due to stress, shock, anger, fear, depression, jealousy, hate etc.

- It helps to bring harmony to situations where there is discord.
- It can help with relationships. To either make or break them, with consideration for what is best for all those concerned, seeing from a wider view. If it is to break then it can also help with the emotions involved.

The distance healing symbol

The third symbol is known as the distance healing symbol.

- This symbol works outside time and space. I still wonder at its effectiveness. It certainly defies logic, which incidentally, it is best not to employ in Reiki.
- As its name implies, it is used to treat people who are not present or near enough to be touched. Nowhere is too far away. It can be used to send Reiki to someone on the other side of the room or on the other side of the planet, or in fact to astronauts, or Martians or whoever.
- It can be used to treat the self, especially useful if you are unable to perform the self-treatment.
- It can be used to send Reiki to parts that cannot be reached.
- It can be activated with just thinking of the person/thing /place, or a photo, a witness (e.g. a piece of hair, nail, their name) can be used, or a proxy patient. (*See* illustration of Toby Bear on page 165 – Dorothy uses him often, and we reckon he glows in the dark now!) Many healers keep either a book or box with peoples names in, to use when they do their daily distance healing session. If I have someone needing intensive treatment then I usually pin their photo or name up somewhere that I pass frequently, and send them a burst whenever I pass. When distant healing was done in the time of Dr Usui, it was called the photograph method, because they only used photographs as their witness. As I mentioned above, a variety of things are now

used to make the link. This is one of the good changes that has come about. Photos were rare in those times, so the distance healing was only available to those who were lucky enough (or rich enough) to have a photograph of themselves. Now it is available to anyone.

- It can be used to connect with the past to help come to terms with events gone by. This can be particularly helpful for those who have suffered abuse, or have feelings of guilt over an event. Those exploring past lives find this symbol useful.

- It can be used to send Reiki to an event or person in the present, e.g. a friend who is having a job interview. You can support them and help them to do their best, while helping the event to go smoothly. We did this with a friend's son, who was going for several interviews – he got offered all of the jobs, despite other formidable applicants.

- You can also send it to the future. Helping plans to run smoothly. Or to an event when you will not be able to do Reiki, or may be distracted, e.g. a visit to the dentist, a job interview, an operation when you will be unconscious. Linear time need not be used, the event is enough to make the link.

- It can also be of comfort to the dying, as it can help to create the bridge between the levels of existence.

- It can help those who have left things unsaid or unfinished when someone dies.

- It can also be of help in house clearing (on an energetic level only that is – Reiki is good, but not that good!).

Feeling doubtful?

If some of these uses seem a bit way out for you don't let that put you off Reiki. Reiki is very versatile. I have listed ways in which fellow Reiki-ists have used the symbols with success, and they come from all walks of life. Use it for what is right for you, and with the intent of the highest good for all those concerned, and you won't go wrong. We don't stop breathing the air, just because others that we don't agree with breath it too, do we?

The Master symbol

The final Sacred Symbol is known as the Master symbol. This is only for use by Masters. Details on its uses are given at the time of initiation.

Preparing Yourself for Initiation into Reiki

I hope that you will look forward to your initiation to Reiki as something special and personal to you. As with any special occasion part of the specialness is in the preparation. You will be joining an ever-growing group of people using Reiki in their lives and for highest good of all.

When you are initiated, your energy body is balanced, energised and enabled to channel Reiki. This may well result in various reactions. Dependant on your physical condition at the time, you may well experience symptoms of a detoxification. (Details in **Limitations and Contra-indications**). This is part of the clearing that prepares you to be a channel to facilitate the transfer of this wonderful energy. The following are things that you *may* choose to implement during the week or so before your initiation (attunement and training). Some will prepare your energetic side, while others will help your physical. Please note that these are only suggestions!

A week before your initiation
No meat

Refrain from eating meat, fowl, or fish for three days or more before. They often carry the residue of chemicals that the animals were given. They will also carry the energies of the animal, which may not be happy ones. (They may include fear, pain, confusion – these can affect you too.) You may also choose to leave out dairy produce and eggs, as they too can carry the animals' energy and contain chemicals. They are also very mucus-forming.

A liquid diet
You could go on a water, fruit or vegetable juice or watery soup fast for the one, two or three days before.
NB. If you are not used to fasting, then do not overdo it.

Reduce stimulant intake
Cut out (or at least reduce) prior to, and eliminate during your training, your intake and use of caffeine, nicotine, stimulants, sugar, sweets and nonessential drugs. These have a detrimental effect on your sensitivity, and cause extra strain on all the systems.
NB. You should not stop taking or reduce any medication without consulting your doctor.

Avoid TVs and computers
Refrain from, or reduce the time you spend, watching TV and sitting in front of VDUs. These emit rays that effect us adversely.

Don't dwell on bad news
Try to avoid listening to, watching or reading bad news. This drags your energies down.

Spend time with nature
Go for quiet walks, spend time with nature, go somewhere beautiful. The wonders and beauty of nature are there to be seen if only you look for them, and are willing to perceive them. Even in cities there is an abundance. It can be found in the most unexpected places. I was throwing stuff into my compost bin, when I saw the hard core of a garlic bulb, the colours ranged from white to pink, and it looked like a flower . . . so start looking!

Practising Reiki

Meditate

Heighten your awareness of the subtle impressions and sensations within and around you.

Meditate every day for the week prior to your initiation. If you are not used to doing this, then take it steady. A few minutes a day. You can build on this. You do not need to execute any fancy techniques, just sit quietly without interruptions and think of Reiki. If your mind interrupts, then just say thanks for the thoughts, send them on their way and return to your thoughts of Reiki. Meditation is a good practice to get into the habit of doing, and here is an opportunity to start.

Release negative thoughts

Release any anger, fear, jealousy, hate, worry or other negative thought patterns that you may be holding on to. Send them to 'the Light' to be reprocessed. The Bach flower remedies can be very helpful here. Create a space around you and fill it with positive and loving thoughts instead.

These suggestions will help not only your physical wellbeing, but will also help to clear your energetic body, making it ready to receive your attunement(s).

NB. If you are unable to instigate any of the above suggestions do not let this put you off doing your training. For instance you may only sign on for your training a day or two before. Remember these are enhancers not compulsory. The choice is yours.

What is a Reiki Master?

A Master is not master *of* or *over* anyone. It is not a position of *power*. In many traditions, not just Reiki, being a Master implied that you were at least a master of yourself, probably having served time with a Master who had also had a Master, with whom he or she had served time, and so on. During that time they would have worked with the Master as a student, observing and being guided so that they attained skills and developed naturally until finally they 'graduated' and were perceived as being well developed, and having been *initiated* into the position of Master. Now in Reiki a person may call themselves a Master as long as he or she has been attuned to the Third Degree and have knowledge of the Master symbol and attunement procedures. So it will be found that there is a wide variance from Master to Master in amounts of experience, self-awareness and growth, knowledge and teaching skills. I would suggest that most of us are still a way off from being master of ourselves in the fullest sense, but that the important thing is that we do recognise this, and work continuously on our own development and experience of Reiki.

For me, a 'Master' is like a parent. Bringing Reiki-life to the child (student), guiding and supporting when needed, until the child makes the move to 'leave home'. A parent should be there for the child, whatever happens, to guide until the child has the skills to make his or her own choices, and then when it is time, to let them go without hindrance, to tread their own life path. As with many a parent/child relationship there is often a time when the child becomes the teacher, even if only for a single instant. My role as a Master brings me many advantages like this, as my 'children' share their experiences with me, enabling me to have vision of life from many different vantage points, which being only one person I can only view from my own position. My students constantly bring me back to base, helping me to review and re-evaluate, and this in itself helps in my personal growth. I look on my privileged position as a Master as an honour, not so much for what *I* do or for who *I* am, but for the work that it enables me to do, in spreading the ability to use Reiki to those who can benefit from it. It gives me much joy and satisfaction, when I get feedback from past initiates telling of how Reiki has changed their lives.

Choosing a Reiki Master

Having made the choice to take a Reiki training course, your next important decision is with which Master you choose to take this life-changing step. There are no rights or wrongs to this. It is horses for courses! The one that is appropriate for you may well not be so for your friend or another person. It is a choice you will need to make for yourself.

With this in mind here are some questions that you may like to consider the answers to, and see which ones feel good to you. In recent years there has been a massive increase of Masters so that in most cases you will be spoilt for choice, so exercise your prerogative and feel 100% good about the person you choose.

Do you resonate well with this person?

This person is going to parent and guide you as you travel your path of Reiki. Your first contact may well be through the post in response to an advertisement. The paperwork may be great, or it may not be quite so good, whichever, it is not always indicative of the Master's ability or personality. I have met several authors whose books I have read and formed a picture of them, only to find they were not as I had pictured them. I had not been making a judgement on them, but I think this illustrates that we all get impressions, from which we make a picture, which my not turn out to be that accurate. Talking with the Master is essential. Ask the Master about his or her path to and with Reiki. How is Reiki integrated into the Master's life? How does he or she present Reiki? Are you going to be comfortable with lots of meditations or would you prefer it to be really down to earth? Ask questions not related to Reiki too. You are going to spend time with this person, you are going to pay the Master for a service and he or she is going to instigate one of the major events in your life. Here you must follow your instincts. If you have any doubts, then look further. Some people travel long distances to be with the Master who is right for them. If you are not too great a distance away, you might even like to book a treatment with this person. If you are unable to have a treatment with the Master you might be able to have one with one of his or her past students. Be aware though that this too may not offer you a true picture, as this person will already be adding a personal touch or two to his or her own practice. Reiki is very special, so start out on the right foot by having the Master that is right for *you*.

Has this Master the experience to teach you?

We all have to start somewhere, but being initiated to the Third Degree does not automatically give the Master wisdom and super knowledge, nor does it magically give the benefits of hands-on experience. It is a bit like driving a car for the first time after you pass your test. You have your license, and now you are on your own and you *really* start to learn about being on the road. Teaching Masters need to have a base of wide experience both in treatment and self development so that they can instruct and support you. Even this does not make them superhuman! But they will be able to give you a good root to grow from, and then the rest will be up to you. In the past Master candidates would do an apprenticeship, working alongside their Master gaining experience until they were ready to fly solo. Some of us still teach this way, so that new Masters have a safety net for as long as they need it, for themselves and their trainees.

What is the Master's lineage?

What is the Master's family tree back to Dr Usui? If it doesn't go back to Dr Usui, then it is not Reiki they are offering. Find out how this lineage presents Reiki. Check how close the Master sticks to this. Again see how comfortable you feel about it.

What form do the classes take?

There are so many forms now, it is not always the one that seems most convenient or that you come across first that is right for you in the long run. Check out the feeling in your heart. What will the course content be? There are some minimum requirements. Will you be spending all your time on Reiki, or will the time be filled up with extras.

How long is the training?

Some Masters offer attunements at Mind/Body/Spirit shows and boom! You're done. Is this what you want? Or would you rather take things a bit slower, and have some instruction and support while giving yourself the time to appreciate and assimilate the energies. Is it over one, two or three days, or is it done in sessions over several days?

How much will it cost?

Cheap is not always a bargain, nor is vastly expensive necessarily the best. Whatever the fee, you need to know that you are getting what you want. You are after a once in a lifetime purchase; it must be the one that is for you.

Find out what the fee covers

Will lunch and handouts be supplied. Will you need to find lodgings? Are there extra charges for ongoing support, certificates?

Is this Master prepared to be there for you after you finish your training?

Will the Master give you a contact number and be available as you grow with Reiki? Some Masters attune and disappear. With modern communications, such as the mobile phone and e-mail, keeping in touch should not be a problem.

Will you receive a certificate?

This is proof of your initiation. If you decide to do your next Degree with a different Master you will need to provide proof of initiation to the previous Degree. You will also need it if you want to take out insurance.

How many people does the Master teach in a single class?

Some Masters only work with small groups enabling them to work on a more personal level, whereas others choose to work with larger gatherings, and some have previous initiates to help them. You may like to be part of an intimate group, or like being part of a large group, or somewhere in between.

Who will initiate you?

Will it be the Master you are talking to, or will it be a trainee, or a helper? Will it be done one to one, or en masse?

How many initiations will you receive?

Generally it is four for the First Degree, and one each for the Second and Third Degree.

Where will the course be held? What facilities will there be?

You may be talking to a Master at home in a rural area, only to find that your course is to be held in a busy city, or vice versa. You may need to check for any allergies that you have, e.g. if you are a hayfever sufferer, then summer in a country area may not be a brilliant choice, if you are sensitive to cigarette smoke it would be worth checking that it will be a no smoking area. Or on the other side of the coin, if you must have a puff or two, will there be somewhere for you to do so? (It would be good if you could go without the weed for your training time! *See* **Preparing Yourself for Initiation**.) Are a map and instructions provided? Is there public transport? Can lifts be arranged?

The bottom line is: make an informed choice but ensure that you are 100% comfortable with it, even if that means waiting until the Master that is right for you appears.

Reiki and Money

This is probably one of the most contentious aspects of Reiki. In the West many feel awkward talking about money– either that or they can't stop!

Dr Usui found that often, if something is given or taken for nothing, it has the possibility of causing the following effects:

- The person receiving the free gift feels obligated and at a disadvantage.
- The person does not fully value the gift.
- The person giving feels taken advantage of.
- The person feels in control of the person who is being given the gift.

So to avoid these there should be some exchange, even if it is what is called an energy exchange. This means that money is not the only acceptable currency. One of the laws of the universe says that you cannot have an action without causing a reaction, e.g. a pendulum cannot continually swing to the left, it has also to swing to the right to maintain its function. If you remove something, then something has to fill the space, albeit just air, or else you create a vacuum. Hence you accept a treatment, value it, show appreciation, remove any obligation to the Reiki-ist, keep the balance. The old maxim might seem appropriate 'Neither a borrower nor a lender be'; or maybe it is more appropriate reworded in a positive way to say 'be both a giver and a receiver'. We need both giving and receiving to keep everything in balance.

Just about everyone has something that they can give. One

lady had nothing material, nor was she physically fit enough to offer a service in exchange, so she asked if she could pray for the Reiki-ist. Exchange beyond value.

Although the above points are valid, it is not good to be too rigid. Common sense and compassion must also be involved. I treated someone in a coma. There was no way that he could give an exchange. So I offered the Reiki, and left it for his higher self to take it or leave it, and I reckon the universe has paid me for him, many times over. Another way of exchange is a LETS system (a form of barter). This enables the participants to have a treatment when they need one, either cashing in credits previously accrued or for the time being getting an 'overdraft'. Within a family or between friends, where often there is an ongoing give and take situation, there is probably little thought of a specific energy exchange. However having said all this, sometimes accepting something for nothing can be a way of giving. *You* are providing the opportunity for that person to give, which may be what he or she needs at that time. So it is not all as simple as it seems – follow your heart, listen to your inner voice and seek out the underlying motive for what you are considering doing. The answer will be within you – you only have to access it – and Reiki itself can help.

There are those who say that Reiki is a gift from God, and therefore should not be charged for. I can understand this. However we all have gifts from God, whether it be a gift of being artistic, clever at sewing, drawing, singing, building, car mending, cleaning, mental agility, management skills, manual skills – these are people's areas of ability, no lesser gifts from God. If still you feel that you should not have to pay for the Reiki, think of paying the water board to deliver drinkable water (another gift from God) to your tap. It costs them in time and expenses. Similarly it costs Reiki-ists their time (a valuable and non-renewable resource), particularly if they make Reiki their life work, they still have to pay their bills, unfortunately – electricity, council tax, food, clothing, car tax etc. do not come free or even for an energy exchange – cash is the only payment accepted. They may also be accumulating expenses related to giving the Reiki, such as heating a room, wear and tear on linen, their treatment bench or in travelling to visit you.

A word about distance healing. The sending Reiki-ists will probably spend quite some time each day sending Reiki to their distance healees, taking phone calls, or dealing with the Reiki mail. This should not be taken for granted, just because no appointment or travelling were involved. Many would be very grateful to receive a realistic donation in appreciation for their part in this very powerful form of Reiki treatment.

In some branches of Reiki, money is used as a symbol of commitment. This is illustrated in the fees that are charged for the training. As an example, some charge $10,000 for the Master initiation (£6,000 in the UK.) This is non-negotiable regardless of the country's monetary status. This sum has not changed since Mrs Takata introduced it as part of Reiki. At the other end of the scale some Masters feel that Reiki should be for everyone, and that it should all but be given away, regardless of their situation.

I come somewhere in between, feeling that there are other ways of showing commitment. Time to a busy person is beyond pounds and pennies, and to someone who has loads of cash, then a few thousand is not going to dent their commitment budget much. However, a reasonable exchange should be made to acknowledge the experience of the initiating Master, their commitment, and the time and expense involved in training someone and of course there should be an expression of honour for the Reiki itself.

Guidelines for Giving a Reiki Treatment

A Reiki treatment should be a pleasure to give and receive. There are many things that can make the difference between an adequate one and one that will leave a Reiki-ist feeling good and a healee looking like the cat that got the cream! If the healee is in the best condition to receive then the Reiki will be utilised to the maximum benefit possible. The following are some points that can enhance a treatment whether it is a professional one or one with a friend.

Getting the healees to where the treatment is going to be done without hassle is a starter. Make sure that they have adequate directions so that they can find you if they have not been before.

A relaxing atmosphere

Being fully prepared for when healees arrive, ensures that they come into a peaceful atmosphere, which may well be an oasis in their busy world. This will immediately give them the chance to start relaxing.

Eat a light meal

Advising them not to feast or fast, eating something light about two hours before will avoid feelings of discomfort for them which they might experience from having either a full or an empty stomach.

Explain Reiki to the healee

Making sure that healees know what Reiki is helps them to make an informed choice about Reiki being appropriate for them. If you are not very good at describing it you could make out an information sheet when you have time to think of what you want to say, and give them a copy of that.

Telling healees what they can expect and what you expect of them, helps to remove any apprehensiveness that they might have. For instance that they will not be required to undress, only to take their shoes and coat off, and loosen any restrictions such as belts or ties that may hinder their comfort.

Make the healee feel at ease

You can help them to feel at ease by giving them some idea of how you are going to proceed, e.g. that you will work the head, down the front of the body, then ask them to turn over, when you will work down the back, and finally end at the feet. But not to move until you squeeze their shoulder which will indicate that you have finished. This way they will feel able to fully relax, and possibly even doze without having to remain alert in case you want them to do something.

Suggesting that they can close their eyes, and that talking is not necessary unless they feel a real need, removes the feeling that they would be impolite if they dozed off, which often happens if they allow themselves to relax fully. If it is a friend you are treating then set aside time to have a chat before or after the treatment.

Good hygiene

Using clean linen or paper for each treatment ensures not only good physical hygiene, but also energetic hygiene too. Sometimes energy can stick after it has been released, and this can affect the next person. If using a pillow then cover it with a small towel. This will help to protect your pillow

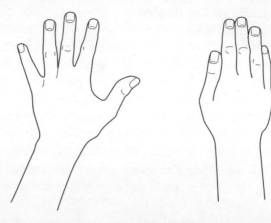

Wrong – fingers open   *Correct – closed fingers and
thumb, relaxed and together*

when they lie on their front. (If they are very relaxed they may dribble! Towels are more absorbent and they don't need ironing.)

Washing your hands before and after a treatment ensures that your hands are not only hygienic but also pleasant to have on the face, especially in the area of the nose and mouth.

Keeping your hands from pressing on the nose and mouth when treating the face ensures that the person does not feel smothered, and can breathe freely. It can also be uncomfortable if the lips are pressed onto the teeth.

Comfortable Reiki treatment

Watch your pressure. People vary in their preferences of pressure, but it is easy to lose your awareness of how heavy you are leaning after you have been standing for a while in one position. Just check it out every few minutes by raising your hands just a minute bit.

Keeping your fingers and thumbs on each hand together in a relaxed manner enables you to focus the Reiki more strongly.

Turning your head slightly to the side while treating the

head can ensure that you are not breathing over the person. Even if you have the sweetest breath, it can be distracting to be sharing someone else's breath.

Removing noisy, dangling, rough or bulky jewellery can prevent it from being distracting or causing discomfort. Watches can sound like Big Ben when near the ear of the healee.

When channelling Reiki it is not unusual for the body and fingers to expand slightly, so removing tight jewellery, and loosening restricting clothing can ensure your comfort. Wearing clothes that are loose and easy to move in, and shoes that are comfy and quiet to move around in are a good idea, better still don't wear any shoes.

Strong smells such as hair sprays, deodorants and perfumes can be unpleasant or at least distracting.

It is a good idea to go to the loo before starting, and offer the healee the option too to prevent having to interrupt the treatment. Reiki often triggers a detoxification, and the desire to go to the loo is one of the reactions. The Reiki-ist is as prone to this as the healee.

Creating a sympathetic environment

Setting up the environment sympathetically can make a big difference to the treatment too. Although Reiki will fit in to any surroundings, we can enhance it by doing a few things. The body can loose heat as it relaxes, so a warm room is a good idea. A blanket to put over them and extra pillows for under the knees can also add to their comfort. Having relaxing music and low lighting and freedom from interruptions will create a peaceful and relaxing atmosphere.

Ending the treatment

When you have completed the treatment and gently awakened a healee, offering him or her a drink of water will help with the detoxification process that may have started, and will also ground the person.

After a treatment, it is to be hoped that healees will be very relaxed. If so they may not be aware that their reflexes and thoughts are likely to be a bit slower than usual. Make them aware of this, and ensure that they are safe to leave and deal with the speed of the world outside, especially if they are driving.

If it is their first Reiki treatment, telling them about the symptoms of detoxification that they may possibly experience will help them to see the symptoms as a positive reaction and remove any worries that they may have had if they did not understand what was happening. (*See* **Possible Reactions to a Reiki Treatment**.) Another information sheet can be useful here as they may not take in what you say, but a handout will be there for reference later on.

If the healee is expecting to stay for a limited time then keeping your eye on the clock will make sure that you do not overrun the allotted time. Giving a treatment that goes with the flow, with no time limits is wonderful, but over-running may mean that a healee has to rush around after, and this will not give the maximum benefit from his or her treatment.

Keep records

Keeping simple records is a good idea. It helps you to keep track of what you have done, and forms a data base of your experiences and re-enforces your learning process with Reiki. You may think that you will never forget something – believe me sometimes the memory is sadly lacking! You can include the reason for treatment, and the reactions of both the healee and yourself and the length of treatment. Date all your entries.

Don't worry the healee unnecessarily

Many healees' first words after a treatment are 'Did you find anything?' Be careful how you answer this. My first experience of reflexology (another therapy that works with energy) gave me three weeks of intense worry. The therapist nearly sent me through the roof when she touched my kidney reflex. 'Better see the doctor about this, your kidneys are awful.' I duly did this, and had tests done. A friend's father had died of kidney failure, so I spent the time between tests and results worrying myself silly in case that was to be my fate too. The tests came back negative. I know now that the kidneys and adrenals are affected by stress, which I was suffering from intensely at the time. The stress was showing in the energetic body, and had not manifested in the physical, nor did it because I took relaxing action to prevent it doing so. So what I am saying is that should you pick up any indications while doing a treatment, don't jump to conclusions, and certainly don't make any diagnosis that you cannot substantiate. If my therapist had been a little wiser she could have said that the energies around the kidney area were reacting to the stress, and I could have been spared a very long three weeks.

Limitations and Contra-indications

Although Reiki is as safe as can be, there are times when it is wise not to use it.

Broken bones
If there is a broken bone, do not apply Reiki until it has been set, as Reiki heals so fast that it may well heal into a mal-union, in which case it will have to be reset. Use it to help speed the healing after it has set. Reiki can pass through a plaster cast.

Pain relief can hinder medical diagnosis
Be aware that Reiki can reduce pain and symptoms, and if going to a doctor this may hinder accuracy in their diagnosis.

Do not use Reiki instead of medical care
Do not use Reiki instead of medical care. For instance, it should never be used to treat a potentially life-threatening condition, such as appendicitis, or to treat a long-term illness in which you are dependent on medication to survive, such as diabetes. However, Reiki could be used as part of a recovery program after an operation or as a complementary therapy.

You should **never** substitute Reiki for a prescribed medication.
NB. You should never stop taking or reduce any medication without the approval of your doctor.

Children and animals

By law, children and animals must receive adequate medical care. Reiki does not count as such, so if either is ill, make sure that they see an appropriate doctor or vet. Reiki can be used to complement any orthodox treatment received.

Anaesthetics

Some suggest that it is best not to use Reiki if someone is under an anaesthetic. This is because Reiki clears chemicals from the body, and so it could reduce the effect of the anaesthetic. However in some hospitals Reiki-ists are working with operating teams, helping to reduce shock and trauma caused by operations, and as the anaesthetist is aware of what is going on, he or she can make the required adjustments.

Everything else comes down to common sense. Reiki is not a cure-all, but as long as you take sensible action when required, it can be of positive assistance in most situations.

Guidelines for Being a Practitioner

Here are some suggestions to help those who have been trained in Reiki, but have not been trained to be a practitioner, to enable them to at least understand some of what they don't know, so that they can either seek the answers from their Master or from another source.

We are lucky in the UK to be able to do hands-on healing without hindrance. In some places you have to be a registered minister, in others it is just not allowed. There is no law that says you may not set up in practice as a Reiki therapist, even with only the First Degree. However there are laws both of the land and moral ones of which you should be aware.

Rules of practice
Unsubstantiated claims
You should not make claims that you cannot substantiate. You should also make sure that no statement you make could be misunderstood, in fact it is often best to state even the obvious, e.g. that you are not medically qualified. Unless you are of course!

You should not work outside of your qualifications, e.g. don't give nutritional advice if you are not qualified to do so.

Limitations
There are some health conditions that you may not treat, and although Reiki is likely to help the person who is ill, it must be *plainly stated* that you are not treating the **condition**.

Some such conditions include cancer, venereal diseases, and notifiable diseases, e.g. typhoid.

Setting up as a business

Local authorities have their own regulations for businesses. Whether this is in a business premises or in your own home. You may need to see about applying for a change of use (your council tax will increase!), they may want to be assured that there is enough parking for your healees, and that your entrance will not be a danger if extra traffic is using it. There may be other regulations that you should find out about.

Music copyright

If you plan to play music you will need a licence to allow you to play music in a place frequented by the public and also one to pay for the artists' copyrights.

Treating children

The law states that children must be given adequate medical care. Whatever your views on orthodox medicine, it is all that is considered to be adequate. So should anyone bring you a child to treat you should make sure the parent/guardian is aware of this, and preferably get a note signed and dated, confirming that you have told them. Obviously if the child is seriously ill you would not hesitate to send them straight to a doctor, but even something less serious should be seen by one too, you can then support the orthodox treatment with Reiki.

Treating animals

Animals must only be treated by vets. However 'hands-on healing' is also allowed, as long as they are also receiving adequate veterinary care. Other complementary treatments are only permitted as long as they are under the supervision of the vet.

Responsibilities

Once you become a practitioner you should also become a professional. This beholds you to various responsibilities:

Insurance responsibilities

You should have practitioner insurance. This should include public liability, professional indemnity and court costs. Although Reiki is as safe as you can get, humans are humans, both the practitioner and patients. Practitioners may make a mistake, patients and their relatives can look for someone to blame. You need to be able to pay up should you make a mistake or if someone has an accident while on your premises. You need to be able to defend yourself should you be accused – especially when you are not in the wrong. You should have court costs included on your policy – preferably unlimited! A limit of one million pounds per claim sounds a lot, but court costs can run up a bill in no time and any successful claim has to be met also. Check this on any insurance you take out. Some give you a total amount of claim, this will include your court costs too, while others offer unlimited court costs on top of the claim amount. You need to inform your household insurers, if you are conducting a business in your home. Should you put a claim in for anything, and they find out you are treating the public (i.e. patients) in your home, this can nullify your insurance. Some practitioner insurers do specific house/clinic and contents policy that take into consideration that you are working from home.

You will also be legally required to pay National Insurance.

Records

You should keep up-to-date and accurate records. This might be needed should you have a claim made against you. You should also be able to get hold of your patients if you need to, e.g. if you had to change their appointment for any reason, or in the event of there being something infectious in your healing room (e.g. scabies, impetigo, German measles – especially for mums to be). This does not necessarily reflect on your hygiene, but it is irresponsible if you are unable to inform those that it may effect. It would also be useful should someone else have to stand in for you at any time. And it helps to consolidate your experience base, and unless you have a brilliant memory it will ensure you have the full picture of any patient, even if he or she hasn't been for some time.

You will be responsible for keeping records for tax purposes. Consult with an accountant about this. A accountant will also be able to advise you as to what expenses you can offset against tax.

Confidentiality
I need hardly say that confidentiality is a must. As a professional you are in a position of trust, and patients have the right to be sure that they can confide in you, should it be necessary, and know that any information they share with you will go no further.

Premises
Hygiene
Premises should be clean and hygienic, including your loo. Enough loo paper, soap and a clean towel should be available.

You should provide clean linen/paper for each patient. This is important, not just for physical hygiene, but on an energetic level too.

You should be fresh and clean, washing your hands between clients. You should be dressed appropriately, i.e. not in jeans and a T-shirt, something a bit smarter is more acceptable. There is no need to wear an overall.

Hazards
You should ensure there are no hazards such as loose carpets for them to trip over or an unsafe treatment bench.

Practising Reiki

You are responsible for the patients' safety and wellbeing while they are with you. So ensure that there are no hazards or risks to their health.

Seek legal advice

If going into business with someone else, or renting rooms to work from, do seek legal advice. There are lots of traps that can be fallen into, even with the most friendly of landlords and associates.

If you are planning to set up in business it is wise to seek further and more in-depth information from an adviser to ensure that you do not come unstuck due to ignorance.

There are more tips under the general guidelines for giving treatments.

Reiki Treatments

Giving a Reiki treatment can be as simple or as complex as you like. Reiki is very versatile, and works well with the minimum of interference.

What a treatment may involve and achieve
Hand positions and sequences
Traditionally a specific set of hand positions is used to give an overall treatment. There are different versions of this sequence, but the variation is not that enormous. Some sequences specifically work on the positions of the chakras, while others work more in alignment with the physical organs or just feed the Reiki in at regular intervals. In reality they overlap on so many things that there is not sufficient difference to make it significant. What is probably more important is the intent and what system (chakras, physical organs or regular input) *you* are choosing to work with. One of the first questions I get asked when teaching reflexology is how it can work when there are so many different versions of the foot map, putting the reflexes for various body parts in different places, and contradicting the areas of other therapies for working with that part. My answer then – and it stands for Reiki too – is that if you use a particular *language*, then that is the one in which the *conversation* (treatment) will be carried out. If your intent is to treat in a particular manner then Reiki will work for you that way.

Practising Reiki

Some Reiki-ists choose not to work with a regular sequence, but use their intuition as their guide. That is OK too, as long as you are sure that you are truly in touch with your intuition and do not end up by missing an important factor. Using a particular sequence, any sequence, regularly is a kind of discipline, in which the same actions are carried out again and again, and again. This in itself creates a powerful energy base to work with. Repetition (practice) hones our skills (makes perfect). When first learning to drive a car, every move had to be thought about, but once the first few lessons have been taken, things start becoming automatic, and we have less chance of making a mistake, or leaving something out. We become skilled at driving. As in anything that is repeated, the familiarity enables us to relax more fully and let the action flow, without interference from our logical mind. In the same way, staying with a particular sequence can help our treatments to flow unhindered and create a space in which our intuition can blossom.

No special state of mind is required to channel Reiki, though being centred makes it a most pleasing experience.

Causes, symptoms and Reiki

Reiki reaches the parts that (some) other therapies don't. It is like water finding its own level, except that Reiki finds the part that is in need and also the cause. To us mere humans with our limited vision, we might just put a sore throat down to an infection (which it might well be), but if there is more to it, then Reiki will find the true cause, which could be for instance connected with something that we should have said and haven't. Reiki can give us the courage to say what is needed, and in the best possible way as well as dealing with the symptom. So it is important to be comfortable with allowing Reiki to do what needs to be done.

Accumulation of Reiki

Reiki has an accumulative effect, and any Reiki is better than none, but if regular treatments are had then the benefits build up. Most people choose to have weekly ones as this fits in with their life styles. If someone has a health problem then between four and six treatments on following days works very well as it gives the body a good strong boost to get on and deal with the ailment. On other occasions it is better to keep to the treatments with a gap of several days or so in between, giving time for everything to adjust. The self-treatment works so well because of the accumulation of Reiki, which helps to keep us vital and protected, reducing the chance of imbalances.

Healing attunements

Healing attunements are given by some Masters. These give the person's system an extra powerful boost of Reiki. With some the person is also enabled to use Reiki for a limited period of time to treat him or herself.

Treating the self

This is the very foundation of Reiki. For both the Reiki-ist and any healee. To give of our best we need to be whole in ourselves, and ensure that we are the best channel for Reiki to come through. If Reiki-ists don't treat themselves they not only hamper their own wellbeing and development, but also they inhibit any treatments that they give to others. These treatments will be fine, but they have the potential to be even better if the Reiki-ist is using Reiki self-treatments. When a treatment is done for someone else, the energy is drawn through the Reiki-ist by the healee, and we get what I call the *milk jug* effect. When you put milk into a jug and then pour it back out, there is always some that sticks to the sides. Well that is what happens in a treatment. That is fine, but as Reiki

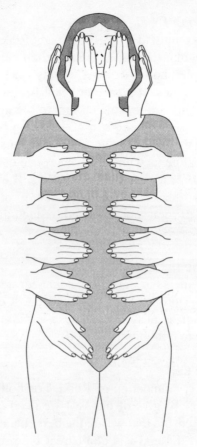

Self treatment from the front

seeks out the parts that need it, and it finds that the Reiki-ist is in need, it will go to the Reiki-ist on the way. From personal experience I notice a massive difference in my treatments, and so do my patients, between when I have been active with my self-treatments and when I have been slack. (Yes, Reiki Masters lapse sometimes too!)

The self-treatment is like a hot bowl of porridge for breakfast

*Self treatment – back view of the head and
shoulders – only carry these out if you can
reach them without strain*

on a winter's morning. It fortifies and energises. It works by
giving what is most needed at a particular time. For instance
if treating at night to sleep, it will help, but if treating in the
morning, it will help the waking process, by brightening and
revitalising. The benefits that initiates get from Reiki are dependent on how they take Reiki into their lives. If they allow
it a free hand then the benefits are limitless. If however they
want to hold it back, it will be patient and wait to be
introduced to new areas.

The self-treatment can be done as part of a getting-up-in-
the morning programme, or a going-to-bed one, or both. It
can be done while riding the bus to work, during a busy day,
even while you are shopping in the supermarket, while in a
meeting, while waiting for someone to turn up, while on the
phone, in fact it fits in wherever you have room for a thought.
Of course setting time aside for the complete session is the
best way to benefit, the rest is really more in the category of
top ups. Those who have put it into their personal care
routines have remarked on the big difference it has made to

their lives. You will see this from some of the reports in **Personal Insights**. We cannot make claims about the powers of Reiki, but the *hearsay* is very convincing.

Ideally, treating the self involves being able to lay your hands on yourself at specific locations, as shown in the diagrams on pages 126 and 127. It is advantageous if a quiet place can be found, where there will be no interruptions for the duration of the treatment. Each position should be held for as long as it feels right. For those who are not sure if they would be able to sense when to move an average is usually between two and five minutes per position. More is fine, particularly if there is a problem there. When people use Reiki regularly, they become sensitive to the feeling of the energy flow, and will just know when it is time to move on to the next position. But to start with, doing it by the clock is fine.

In a self-treatment, the front positions are all that are needed. However if you are able to treat the back positions without strain, then it is good to include these too. If you have been initiated to the Second Degree then you can use the distance symbol to treat the back positions, or any other bits that you are not touching. An instance would be if you have a bad foot, and you didn't feel comfortable stretching down and holding it. Remember Reiki spreads out within the body to where it is needed, so, if you have a bad back or foot, feeding Reiki to the front positions will affect them too. However it feels really good to have Reiki going directly on to the poorly part, and there is no harm in giving Reiki a helping hand.

Sometimes setting up a new routine is not easy, and compromises have to be made, to coax it into place. For those who think that sitting still for anything up to an hour would be impossible, I suggest that the time taken to do a treatment is kept to a comfortable duration, for instance two minutes per position, and building the time up to the five minutes or so for each as it all becomes more familiar. Combining it with an activity that enables sitting down for a while, e.g. watching TV can also help. This is not ideal, but each journey starts with a single step, and Reiki is very adaptable. Even sitting around with family and friends gives us the opportunity to do some self-treatment. They might find it a little distracting to have you holding your head for the first three positions, but the other positions could be done in company and the remainder done at another time.

Getting started

Probably the hardest thing about self-treatments is getting into the habit of doing them. It is so much easier to help others than to take time for ourselves. But we do need to. After an initiation to Reiki there is the twenty-one-day clearing period. During this time there is often an increase in energy and enthusiasm, and so this is a good time to introduce it to your routine. (Interestingly, twenty-one days is the time period recommended by many of the habit breaking and reprogramming courses offered widely now. If you keep up the twenty-one days then you have got over the worst part of starting a new regime. Dr Usui also took twenty-one days for his fast and retreat.) The Reiki self-treatment itself is a wonderful support to aid you through the balancing and detoxification that may also take place, during these twenty-one days. So there is really lots of incentive to get going. As you will see in the training section, I set a lot of store by the self-treatment, and encourage my students to get stuck in straight away. Once you have used it regularly, you will not *want* to do without it.

Keep going

If you can find a regular slot for your self-treatment, then it is much easier to keep up the discipline. I usually do a session before I get up in the morning, and another when I go to bed at night. This one usually doesn't get completed, though I am sure Reiki finishes it off for me, as I sleep very well. I also do impromptu top-ups through the day too. If I am not using my hands I place them on myself anywhere that I can without drawing undue attention to myself, maybe on my thigh if I'm sitting, or resting it across my body if standing. I call the Reiki, and off we go. The benefits that result are enough incentive to keep on treating regularly. Remember this is not a selfish thing, it is caring for the self and each of us is special and worthy in our own way. Then if you are called upon to help others you are well primed to care for them too.

Be comfortable

You will have gathered self-treatments can be done any time, anywhere, sitting, lying, standing. Some people find it uncomfortable to put their hands up and around their heads

Self treatment – being comfortable

and hold for some time, as the position can make their arms ache. If the treatment is being done sitting up, the first and Second position can be made more comfortable by placing a pillow under the upper arms and across the chest. This wedges the arms up and supports them. The elbows can also be rested on the knees. If lying down on the back, then use a pillow again as above, i.e. tucked underarm and over the chest, or if lying on your side the elbows lend support to each other.

Do it in company

There is no need to make a big fuss about doing your treatment. If you want a top-up, or got up late and missed your usual time, then you can do a discreet session. If you are with people who know what you are doing, and in a place where it is all right to be unconventional, then it is fine to do it. There appears to be a thing we call *passive Reiki*. This is the overflow of Reiki from a treatment, which reaches those around, so your friends may well benefit too. I have found this most noticeable when I have been doing a talk on Reiki, and if I am doing a demonstration. The audience all start struggling to keep their eyes open. No it is not boredom! It is just that they are picking up the Reiki, and relaxing deeply. I proved this by doing demonstrations of Reiki (during which it is easy to talk) while I was talking on another subject that I knew people were interested in. The same thing happened – people kept dozing off! They didn't if I talked only on the other subjects.

Others that sense the passive Reiki are pets. Mine like to be with me as much as possible, but if I am doing a self-treatment around them, they want to be as near to the source as possible, and the effect on them is noticeable.

Making the commitment to yourself to do self-treatments is so worthwhile. Any Reiki is better than no Reiki, so if you only have a few minutes, use them. Regular treatments have an accumulative effect so it really is a good *habit* to cultivate.

Treating others

Treatments can be simple and last only minutes or can be more in-depth and last for hours, depending on the situation and the reason they are required. On a first aid level, for either the self or another, just placing a Reiki hand on or over the affected part for a few minutes may be all that is needed. Or, if a more in-depth treatment is required, then the healee will need to be either sitting or lying down, and the duration will normally be around 40 minutes to an hour long, though this can vary greatly. Whichever sequence you choose, an aid to memorising the sequence is if you divide it into three sections. The head and throat or upper chest, (positions 1–4), from the chest down, (positions 5–8) and then the back, (positions 9–12). Each position is usually held for between two and five minutes each. This may vary from position to position. If you are new to treating with Reiki, start with shorter treatments to build up your 'stamina' until you get used to it and feel happy doing a longer one. Turning it into an endurance test will not benefit anyone, and may in time put you off ever starting to do a treatment. The seated treatment only has eight positions as it combines positions 5–8 with positions 9–12, and so this will obviously take less time to do.

Seated treatments

Seated treatments are very easy to give as you require very little space, and they can be given whilst life carries on around you, without causing a disruption. As you will find described in other parts of this book they can be done in the middle of business situations, in classes and at talks, in fact anywhere that you can sit someone down. They are ideal for those who cannot lie down, or for anyone who is in a wheelchair, (Reiki can pass through it). It is also suitable for pregnant women when they get large, and lying down becomes uncomfortable for them.

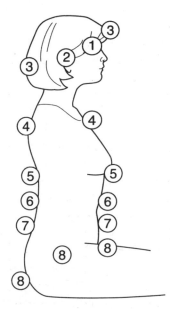

Treating others – the positions for seated treatment

Something to remember however is that healees receiving the treatment may well relax deeply, and so it is a good idea to have something for them to lean against, should they feel they need to slump. This could be a desk or a table, or even the back of the chair if you sit them back to front in it. Whatever you choose, make sure that it is secure and well padded, ideally with a pillow or cushion, but coats, blankets and towels all serve well in an impromptu situation. I have been involved in doing treatments at exhibitions in some of the noisiest and most unlikely places, for instance in an area at the top of a set of escalators in a busy shopping centre. We had more people wanting treatments than we had treatment benches so we were doing them with the people sat on chairs. Despite the noise of the shoppers and the generally 'busy' atmosphere many of the healees dozed off even though they were sitting rather than lying. Lots of people took the chance to try Reiki out, many of whom were sceptics, and even they found that they could not keep their eyes open, as they relaxed. We had many converts that day.

To give a seated treatment

- Find somewhere for the healee to sit. This could be the floor, but a chair or stool is usually more comfortable.
- Make sure there is somewhere for the person to rest forward onto, should he or she relax and need support.
- Have the support padded so that it is comfortable for the healee to lean against.
- Start by standing behind the healee with your hands on his or her shoulders. This is to allow you both a moment of peace to connect and relax into the coming treatment. Taking a few deep breaths can help too.
- You may want to say a prayer, or ask for some help and guidance, or just to take a few moments to ask for Reiki to

Make sure the patient is comfortable

come through, and to establish its flow before moving on to the treatment proper.

- Each position is usually held for between two and five minutes, unless you feel otherwise.
- Stand behind the person, gently placing your hands over his or her eyes and cheeks (position 1). It is a good idea to support the person yourself at this point, just by resting the side of your body against the healee's back, because he or she may already be relaxing, and while you are treating the head the healee cannot lean forward.
- Next you move your hands over the ears and sides of the head (position 2).
- Then moving to your right, (if this is not possible going to your left is fine) put your right hand over the brow/third eye and your left around the back of the head at the base of the skull/alta major (position 3).
- You may choose to treat the throat, or move onto the upper chest and back (position 4). This completes the first part, and the person can now relax forward if they want to.
- You may need to sit, kneel or stoop down for the rest of the positions to prevent strain on your own back. If you are planning to kneel, then try and have something soft to kneel on.
- Place your right hand on the solar plexus/around the lower end of the ribs and the diaphragm and the left hand on the back at roughly the same level which will cover the adrenals (position 5).
- Next move lower on the front and back at about waist level (position 6).
- Then lower again to cover the sacral chakra/ reproductive organs and intestines (position 7).
- Position 8 is almost impossible to reach with the person sitting, especially if the person is leaning forward so it is often done by moving around to the person's back again, and by placing a hand on each of his or her hips.

- Arms and legs can also be treated – *see* **Treating the arms and legs** on page 144 – following instructions for prone treatments.

After the treatment is finished you may like to give thanks for the gift of Reiki, and also to seal the person's energy body to contain the Reiki for his or her use, and to close the healee's chakras which will have opened to receive it. Many Reiki-ists do not feel this is necessary, however it is something that I like to do as, quite apart from anything else, it rounds off the end of the treatment nicely. All I do is put my hands together over the healee's head, then part them and draw lines down to the floor, one down the front and one down the back of the body about two inches away from the healee. I then repeat, having moved a quarter of a turn round them, so that I can draw lines down his or her sides. This forms a kind of wigwam. I then gently squeeze the healee's shoulder to indicate that the treatment has ended. I then give the healee a glass of water to help bring him or her back to full alertness.

Prone treatments

Probably the most popular way of giving a Reiki treatment is for healees to be lying down. Ideally a treatment bench is used, as this puts them at a comfortable height for Reiki-ists to work on them. However if a treatment bench is not available there are lots of alternatives, and here are a few suggestions. If you have a sturdy dining table, then, with a few folded blankets or a duvet, it can be made quite comfortable. Likewise a door or planks of wood suspended on trestles or other supports. Beds are OK too, or piles of pillows and cushions on the floor, but both of these can put a strain on the Reiki-ist's back as they hold the positions.

If you want to have a bench of your own but find you cannot afford it, try your local hospitals and clinics. They sometimes have old equipment for sale at extremely favourable prices.

Watch out for adverts on your health shop notice board or the classified ads, or even advertise your requirement. There seems to be quite a trade in Second-hand benches.

Treating someone else can be as pleasurable for the Reiki-ist as it is for the healee, and there are a few things that can help to make this so. Reiki will flow whatever, but the experience can enhance the way in which healees makes use of it, how receptive they are and how they mentally perceive the treatment given. When people experience something pleasant it makes them feel good, so their whole is more likely to be in harmony and therefore their 'being' will have been enhanced totally. However if they have experienced a happening that had an agitated feeling to it, then this is probably how they will feel afterwards, and certainly not in a state of peace and harmony.

The primary considerations are that both the healee and the Reiki-ist are comfortable and at ease. The environment, equipment, clothing and attitudes of both parties will affect this state. You will find tips under **Guidelines for Giving a Reiki Treatment**. Here are a few additional ones that will apply especially to treating someone who is lying down. If you are treating someone on the floor you will have to make the best of it, as this does create a strain on the back. However if it is someone that you would normally cuddle with, then lying beside him or her and adapting the hand positions can work well.

Preparation for a prone treatment

- If treating on a treatment table ensure that it is at the right height to enable you to stand straight with your hands in front of you, resting on the healee, without having to stoop at all.
- Get the healee to lie with his or her head right up to the top end of the bench, but not hanging over it. If you have a wide surface for the healee to lie on, have them come close to the side you will be standing on, so that in both cases

you don't have to stretch over to reach the person. As each person will be different in size you may find that whatever surface you use there will be some treatments where the healee is too high, or too low. By adding or removing some folded blankets, foam, pillows etc. a few inches can be added or lost. Ideally an adjustable height treatment table is the answer.

- If you choose to sit while giving a treatment you also need to ensure that you have a seat that enables you to sit comfortably while maintaining the treatment position without fidgeting. Having something soft to rest your arms on helps. Positions 1 and 2 on the head, and 4 either around the throat or on the upper chest, are done by being at the head and looking down towards the feet. Resting the arms on the pillow relieves any strain. Be careful not to catch the healee's hair. Position 3 is done by cupping the head in the hands so you will want to be sitting high enough so that you do not strain the undersides of the wrist.

- When moving to the side, if you are sitting, putting a pillow along the side of the healee's body provides a soft surface to support and cushion your arms, and it absorbs any pressure that might have discomforted the healee.

- If you choose to do your treatment standing, you will, for the most part, be standing still, and this, even when doing Reiki, can bring about discomfort and the fidgets, which may well prevent you from experiencing the bliss that can come, and even disrupt the peace for the healee. It doesn't matter whether you use your left or right hand on any particular position, as Reiki has no polarities, but by moving them in a specific and synchronised way you can firstly help the treatment sequence to flow with grace, which will add to the overall harmony, and secondly reduce any discomfort for you that may arise from being virtually static.

To give a prone treatment

- Get the healee to lie down on his or her back. Put a shallow pillow under the head. (The pre-shaped foam ones are very useful, as they make getting to the third position much easier, as there is a dip along which to slide the hands into place.) The person may find it more comfortable if another pillow is placed under their knees as well, removing strain on the spine.

- Tell the healee what you are going to do, where you will be touching, or not touching if you choose to work above the body. Arrange a signal for getting him or her to turn over, usually a squeeze on the arm and agree where the pillows need to be moved to, i.e. the one under the knees will need to be moved down to the lower leg to support the ankles and remove any strain on the knees. Also the pillow under the head, may be better if it is either removed or moved down to the upper chest, otherwise the healee could end up with his or her head twisted too far round and then not be able to breathe freely or be just plain uncomfortable. An end-of-treatment signal should also be arranged, usually a squeeze on the shoulder. All this enables the healee to relax fully into the treatment without having to consider what you will be expecting him or her to do. Healees can observe, with a very low level of awareness, what is happening, knowing what will be next, and what they have to do.

Make the patient comfortable with small pillows

Practising Reiki

- Try to avoid talking to the healee during the treatment as this can raise the alertness levels, and dispel the really deep levels of relaxation that can be reached.

- Put a light blanket over the healee, as the body can lose heat as it relaxes, and feeling chilly will also affect comfort and the ability to fully enjoy the treatment. You are more likely to feel hot, so you need to be aware of both your needs and meet them.

- So you have the patient lying down, experiencing some T.L.C. (tender loving care), already beginning to relax, ready to take in the Reiki. Position yourself at the head of the bench, and place your hands gently over the front of his or her shoulders. This is just to give you both time to connect, to centre and focus your intent, and to say any prayer or request that you may feel appropriate. (You may choose to do this either silently or vocally.)

- When moving your hands from position to position try to keep one hand in touch with the healee's body at all times, by moving one hand to the next position and then joining it with the other. This eliminates any element of (minor) shock that could be experienced if the healee is dozing, and loses track of where you are.

  Although the illustrations show working from moving to your right, I will refer in the text to *head* and *foot hand*, rather than left or right, so that it can be read with meaning whichever side you are on. The head hand being that which is nearest to the head when you stand at the side (the left hand in the diagram), and the foot hand being nearest to the foot (the right hand in the diagram). The foot hand is always moved first, eliminating any crossing over and clumsy movements. You should not cross your legs, ankles or arms when treating. You should also discourage the healee from doing so.

Treating the front

Position 1

When you feel yourself ready to start, and the Reiki is flowing, then place your hands over the healee's eyes and cheeks, being careful not to squash the nose or press on the mouth. In this position you are starting the treatment of the head, which of course houses the senses and the brain, from which signals go to all over the body, so in a way you are already in touch with all of the body. You are also affecting the crown and brow/third eye chakras which are in the head.

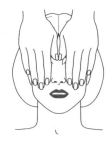

Position 1

Position 2

When moving one hand, then the other, to the sides of the head and over the ears, again you are treating the head and all its parts, and more specifically the two sides of the brain and the ears, which are about hearing and balance.

Position 2

Position 3

Gently roll the head slightly to one side, and ease the hand on the other side under it, roll the head to the other side, and put the other hand under. Here you are treating the brain and brain stem, the bit that joins the mental to the physical, also the back of the brow chakra.

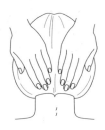

Position 3

Position 4
Carefully lowering the head, move one hand followed by the other either to the chin and throat and throat chakra (be careful not to press onto the Adam's apple) or to the upper chest. As Reiki spreads anyway, whichever you choose will affect the other.

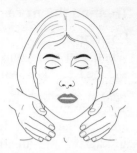

Position 4

Position 5
Move around to the side of the body resting what will be your head hand lightly on the shoulder just to maintain contact. Then either place your foot hand fingers pointing upward toward the face, along the breast bone, and the head hand across the fingertips to form a 'T', treating the heart and upper lungs and the heart chakra. Or putting your head hand forward onto the further side of the body, and the foot hand nearer to you near up to the bust line, over the lower lungs. This also treats the heart chakra. This may be comfier for those who may feel that the other position is a bit too intimate.

Position 5

Position 6
Now this is where the care for the Reiki-ist comes in. When you move to this next position move the foot hand first to the side away from you, then move the head hand to the side nearest you. (Do you see what has happened? You have changed your skeletal and

Position 6

muscular stance, thus reducing stress on the whole structure of your body.) In this treatment position the lower lungs, spleen, liver, stomach, pancreas, gall-bladder and solar plexus chakra of the healee are being focused on

Position 7
When ready to move on to this next position, move the foot hand first to the side nearest you, and then the head hand to the far side. This position covers the intestines, pancreas, reproductive organs and sacral chakra.

Position 7

Position 8
Position 8 is a 'V' shape starting with the foot hand forming the far side, and the head hand the near side. As this is an intimate area the 'V' can be formed by resting the thumb side of the head hand against the top of the near side leg, and the little finger side of the foot hand against the top of the one on the far side. The fingers of the head hand are pointing to the narrow end of the 'V' as is the wrist end of the foot hand, thus forming a 'V' over the crotch. This covers the base chakra, and the exits of elimination. Note: if you don't start off with the correct hand applications at the beginning of the sequence you will end up with an 'A' shape instead of a 'V' when you get to this position.

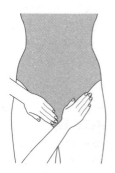

Position 8

Practising Reiki

This completes the front of the body unless you need to work any other specific parts. If the person is unable to lie on their front then the treatment can be finished off here, or by spending some time holding the feet as an extra position, before sealing them

Treating the arms and legs

If you want to treat the arms and legs, now is a good time to do them, as most people are more comfortable lying on their backs than their fronts. Arms and legs are optional, as they are affected by the energy put into the torso anyway, but sometimes it is appropriate to do them, especially if they have been under any extra strain, and certainly if you have the time, they are a pleasing addition. The method of treating them will depend on how much time is available, and their requirements, but here are a few options. The positions that may be considered are the joints (hips, knees, ankles, feet and toes/shoulder, elbow, wrist and hand) and the muscles (thigh and calf/upper

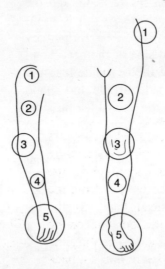

Treating the arms and legs

arm and lower arm). If very little time is available then treating the legs by just holding the hip with one hand and the foot with the other will cover the whole limb. Similarly the shoulder and hand for the arm. You may choose to treat the joints only, or the muscles only, or joints and muscles ending by holding the foot or hand. The legs can be treated together by placing a hand on each leg at the same time, or each position on alternating legs using both hands on each leg, or by treating all the positions on one leg with both hands and then repeating on the other leg. The arms can be treated in the same way but are generally best treated one then the other, as to do them bit by bit alternately would mean you would have to keep going from side to side of the body, which could be disruptive. Arms and legs can also be incorporated into the sitting treatment.

Treating the back

Make the patient comfortable on his or her front

Position 9

The ninth position is over the 'wings' or shoulder blades. This can be done by either standing behind the head and pointing the hands towards the feet, or from the side with the head hand on the further side, and the foot hand on the nearer. This position is treating the upper lungs and heart, and the back of the heart chakra.

Position 9

145

Position 10

Moving the foot hand first to the further side and the head hand to the nearer, the hands are covering the lower lungs, kidneys, adrenals and back of the solar plexus chakra.

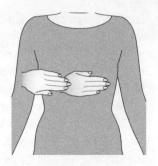

Position 10

Position 11

Moving the hands in sequence as before, foot hand nearer and head hand away, they come to rest just below the waist line. This covers the lower back and sacrum, also the sacral chakra.

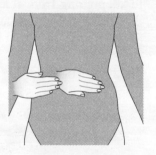

Position 11

Position 12

The final position is at the base of the spine and can either be a 'V' or a 'T'. The 'V' is formed in the same way as it was on the front, the open end facing toward the healee's head, with both hands flat onto the buttocks. If using a 'T' then the head hand forms the cross and the foot hand covers the coccyx with the fingers pointing up towards the spine. (This position is excellent for haemorrhoids.)

Some Reiki-ists like to return to the position at the back of the head here, standing at the top of the body with both hands resting on the head with the fingertips on the occiput (base of the skull).

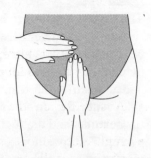

Position 12

Ending the treatment

- Some Reiki-ists just move to the feet and hold until they feel ready to let go.
- Others do the *Takata Stroke*, which involves holding the top of the spine (and the clothing at the neck to stop it bunching) with the head hand, and then using the first two fingers of the foot hand, one either side of the spine, do a sweeping stroke from the top of the spine to the sacrum, three times and then with the palm of the foot hand on the sacrum gently rock the person. This can be an effective way of starting to bring them back to reality, as it stimulates all the nerves coming from the spine, and also runs along meridians.

As I mentioned earlier, a sequence for sealing the person's energy field and grounding them makes an appropriate finish to the treatment:

- Take the right hand and drawing three ovals around the person, starting at the top of the head and passing under the feet in an anticlockwise direction, keeping the palm of the hand facing inwards at all times, and avoiding any pleats in the oval. These ovals seal in the energies. When the third oval had been completed at the crown, a line is made down the centre of the body with the palm of the hand floating about two inches above it, starting at the crown, going over the head and all the way down to the feet. This line helps to ground the person, aiding them to return to reality. The feet can then be held for a while, and brushed off just the once to finish.
- A squeeze on the shoulder indicates the end of the treatment.
- A glass of water is a good idea, as it helps in grounding the person as well as aiding the detoxification process, which may also have induced a thirst.

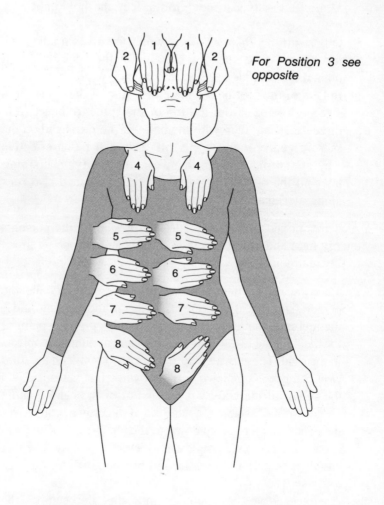

For Position 3 see opposite

A possible arrangement for treatment of the front

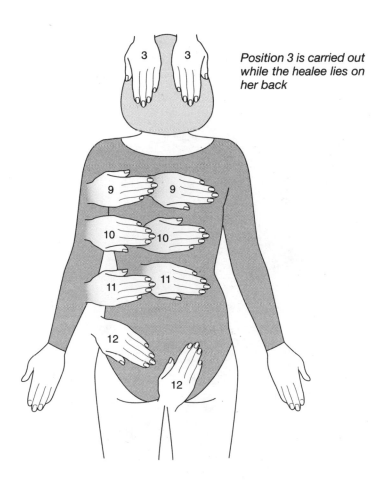

*Position 3 is carried out
while the healee lies on
her back*

A possible arrangement for treatment of the back

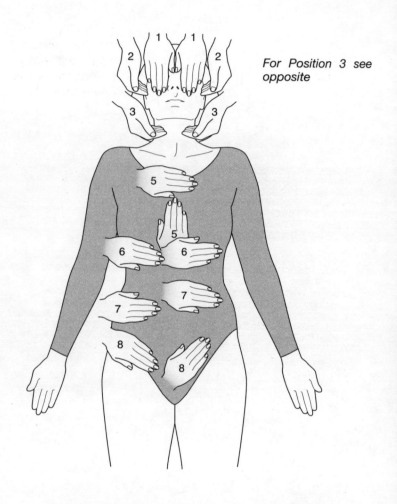

For Position 3 see opposite

A possible arrangement for treatment of the front

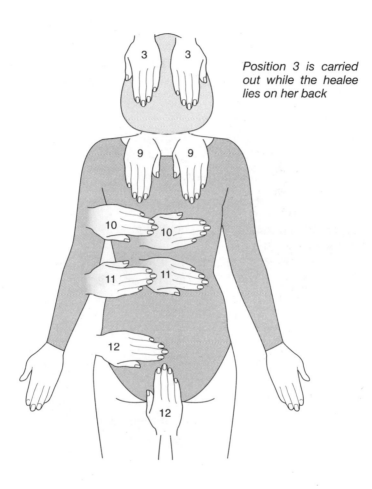

Position 3 is carried out while the healee lies on her back

A possible arrangement for treatment of the back

Distance Healing

This is a versatile and logic-defying way of treating a subject that is not present. This includes people, animals, and other living things, incidents (past, present and future), and inanimate objects.

It was originally called the 'Photograph Method', because, as mentioned previously, a photograph was used to make the connection with the healee.

To perform Reiki distance healing Reiki-ists needs to have been initiated to the Second Degree of Reiki. In this Degree they receive the Sacred Symbol that enables them to create a strong link that will carry the Reiki through time and space. It is useful for Reiki-ists to be able to offer daily support between hands-on treatments, and also to treat without hindrance no matter where a subject is. There is no need to even know the person, let alone to meet or be with him or her. I have quite a few patients who I have never met. Both the following examples live hundreds of miles away from me. One I only corresponded with by letter for over a year, until we finally spoke on the phone to arrange a meeting during a holiday in my area, while another phoned regularly to keep me informed of his condition, and we only met eventually due to our coincidental meeting in a particular place miles away from both our homes at the same time. Living at the other end of the UK from my family, the distance healing enables me to still be able to help when needed. Using Reiki distance healing also alleviates that awful feeling of being helpless when confronted with some of the awful news we hear about. When sending unsolicited Reiki it should always be added 'that it is sent for the good of all those concerned' and as we may not be privy to what that is we leave it to Reiki and the Creator to know best.

Receiving distance healing

There is no need for the healee to know the time that the healing is being transmitted to them. Yet it can be very pleasant to be aware of receiving the Reiki. If the Reiki-ist is able to set a specific time for the sending, and let the healee know, then the healee can sit quietly, ready to receive and, if sensitive to feeling the Reiki, get a very similar treatment sensation to that of a hands-on one. The advantage of being aware is that the healee can participate in the treatment, rather than just going along without any involvement. Some people like to make a special moment out of it, by finding a space and creating an appropriate atmosphere, such as by playing some relaxing music and lighting a candle.

Those that are sensitive to *feeling* the Reiki can often tell when it is being sent to them, whatever the time. When I have had a very needy patient, I have suggested that the patient thinks of me should he or she need an extra boost. Having created the link between us with the distance healing symbol, I have been aware of such requests, as the person will pop into my mind, unbidden from my end. Sometimes it works in reverse. I will get a prompt out of the blue, to send Reiki to someone, and the person has been aware of the Reiki coming through. We have confirmed times with each other after the event. Please note that I did not send the Reiki unasked for, as I had an agreement with the person to support with Reiki whenever needed.

The real proof of distance healing for me has been when treating animals. They do not experience the placebo effect, and yet feedback from their owners suggests that they received the Reiki when it was being sent, usually going quiet and restful until they had had enough, and then moving off, which often coincided with me feeling the flow of Reiki stopping. After receiving Reiki from a distance, animals have manifested improved energy levels, condition and interest in life. These occurrences were not one-off happenings, their regularity confirmed them.

Sending distance healing

It should be noted that just because neither the sender nor the receiver sense the Reiki flowing, it does not mean that it is not happening. Things like tiredness, stress, chronic illness, passing ailments, e.g. a cold will all help to deaden the senses.

For those who have been initiated to the First Degree only, they can still give Reiki-help to those who are not with them, though not quite so instantly. They can charge a quartz crystal by holding it in their hand and 'treating' it with Reiki. Crystals are open to being 'programmed'. The crystal can then be sent to the person needing the help and the person can either carry it with him or her or be more specific and place it against the area needing the healing. Dr Usui used to charge crystals and use them in this way.

To send a quick energy boost or supportive burst of Reiki then it can be as simple as just using the distance healing Sacred Symbol along with the thinking of who or whatever it is that is to receive it. This can be very useful when you get a phone call in the middle of a busy day. But to take time to do a proper full length treatment is more beneficial.

In Dr Usui's time, treatments were for people only and a photograph was used to make the link with them. But many years later we have expanded the uses of this symbol. The initial format remains good though, and sending distance Reiki can be very rewarding.

Each Reiki-ist will have their own ritual for sending, and here are a few suggestions:

Toby Bear

- Create for yourself a space. This does not have to be away from company, but you should be able to withdraw and relax. Relaxing music, lighting a candle, and a nice place to be is a bonus. Then using the symbols, focus your thoughts on the object of your treatment.
- Have a photo, write their name on a piece of paper, have something of theirs to help *you* focus on them, and cup this in your hands.
- Have a teddy or doll to use as a proxy patient and treat it as though the person were present with you. (*See* the picture of Toby Bear, author, travelling companion of Dorothy and professional proxy patient!)

155

Practising Reiki

- If you can visualise, then you can imagine them without any connectors.

These treatments usually last from 15–30 minutes. This is fine to do if you only have one or two people to treat daily, but if you have any more (or lots more!) then it's not really a viable option. But of course there is a way to do it:

- Write everyone's name in a book or on a card and keep it in a special box. Then instead of holding just one person in your hands to treat at any one time, you can hold the book or box and send Reiki to all of them all at once. You may like to run your eye over the names before starting your healing, but again this depends on the number you have.
- Should you be unable to hold your 'names' then you can just ask that Reiki be sent to all those in 'my healing box/book' while thinking of it in you mind's eye, and this makes the connection.
- If you are wanting to send Reiki to an event, place or similar, then you can use an identifier in the same way as the names. You do not need to know where a person is to send them Reiki. People are a bit like mobile phones. They each have a unique 'number' and Reiki will find them wherever they are, because there are no bad reception areas with Reiki!

The Physical Body

The following is a brief description of the various parts of the physical body, and how they function. It is far from complete in its content, but I hope it will serve as a point of reference while reading this book, and maybe stimulate your interest in how your body works. Should you want to know more I suggest that you investigate further, possibly in anatomy and physiology books designed for nurses, as these are written in plain language which is easy to understand. Or there are some correspondence courses teaching basic anatomy and physiology which are inexpensive and very flexible.

I am starting with the five senses, as these are generally all treated at the beginning of a Reiki session. They are our sensors with which we perceive the world about us.

The skin
This is our organ of touch. Touch is of great importance to our happy and healthy survival. Sadly our society does not fully approve of being too tactile with each other. Research is showing that touch is very important for us all for our health and wellbeing. The skin is also the 'great eliminator', it rids our bodies of waste products (by sweating). It is the largest organ of the body.

The eyes
The eyes are our window to the world. They have a complex and detailed structure, which when healthy adjusts our focus

and controls the amount of light that enters to give us optimum vision of all about us.

The nose

The nose funnels air up to our olfactory nerve, enabling us to smell what is about us, it also filters and warms the air giving it the proper Degree of moisture before it enters the lungs. It is capable of recognising 4,000 different scents. Our sense of smell can also affect our sense of taste.

The mouth and tongue

The mouth and tongue give us our sense of taste and starts the process of digestion. The tongue has sensors on that can recognise the difference between sour, salty, bitter and sweet. When these tastes are encountered they set off the production of saliva which starts the break down of food, before it goes on to the stomach to be digested.

The ears

The ears not only feed back sounds to us, so that we can hear what is going on around us and give us information, but they also affect our balance. The ear is made up of three parts:

1 the external or outer ear
2 the middle ear
3 the inner ear

The outer ear acts like a satellite dish, registering all the sounds and feeding it back onto the ear drum (tympanic membrane). This acts like a drum in an orchestra. The sound is like the drum sticks, setting the drum skin in motion. The sound waves are magnified by twenty-two times as they pass to the middle ear via three bones called the anvil, hammer and stirrup. The inner ear is not only used for hearing. It also performs the function of keeping balance. This is done by semicircular ducts filled with a fluid called endolymph. There is one canal that registers upward and downward motion, another forward motion, and yet another for lateral or sideways motion. The fluid moves around as we move and tiny hairs detect this and send messages to the brain, so that it can get the body to make necessary adjustments to keep itself upright. The pressure in the middle ear is equalised with air coming from the outside through the Eustachian tubes which run from the middle ear to the pharynx. When we get colds, infections of the ear or even sore throats all this can be affected.

The sinuses

The sinuses are also covered in the head positions. These are air cavities in the bones of the face. They act as filters when we breathe in air through the nose. They also give resonance to the voice. These spaces in the bones of the face help to lighten the weight of the head, lessening the stress on the neck.

The endocrine system

The endocrine system consists of the pituitary gland, the thyroid gland, the parathyroid glands, the thymus gland, the suprarenal or adrenals glands, the reproductive glands and the pancreas. This is a system of ductless glands which produce hormonal secretions that pass directly into the blood, and regulate the body functions, including growth, metabolism and activity. They have a big effect on both the mental and emotional states as well. These glands are spread throughout the body as you can see from the diagram. (*See* figure on next page.)

The pituitary gland

The pituitary gland works with the hypothalamus (which is not classed as an endocrine gland, but is part of the brain). The pituitary gland is often called the Master gland as it regulates the actions of all the other glands. It lies between the eyes and behind the nose.

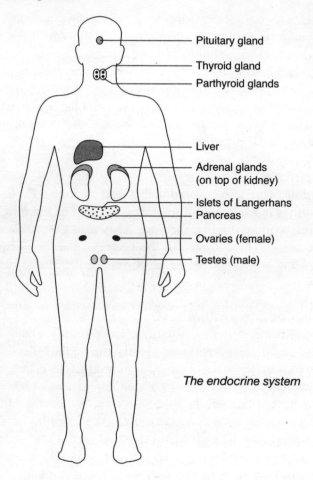

Pituitary gland

Thyroid gland

Parthyroid glands

Liver

Adrenal glands
(on top of kidney)

Islets of Langerhans

Pancreas

Ovaries (female)

Testes (male)

The endocrine system

The pineal gland

The pineal gland is about 1 cm long and is located in the fore-brain. This gland secretes, among others, a hormone called melatonin which it is thought has an effect on our moods. (Research is showing that it may be connected with Seasonally Affected Disorder, relating to the amount of daylight experienced.)

The thyroid gland

The thyroid gland has two lobes and is found either side of the trachea with the two sides joined by an isthmus. Each lobe is about 4 cm long and 2 cm across. It secretes thyroxin and tri-iodothyronine and regulates growth and general metabolism. The thyroid has a big effect on our mental wellbeing.

The parathyroid glands

There are four of these glands, two lying behind each lobe of the thyroid gland. They secrete parathormone which raises the blood calcium and maintains a balance between the calcium and the phosphorus content in the blood and bones.

The thymus gland

The thymus gland lies in the lower part of the neck and is a maximum length of 6 cm. From puberty on this gland begins to atrophy. It is thought that its secretions put a brake on the development of the sex organs, so as it atrophies they can continue to develop. The thymus is also believed to play an important part in the immune system by producing T-lymphocytes.

The suprarenal or adrenal glands

There are two of these glands, they are yellow and triangular-shaped. They are found one each on top of the kidneys. They are divided into two parts each. The cortex, produces corticosteroids, which control the sodium and potassium balance, stimulate the storage of glucose and affect or supplement the production of sex hormones. The medulla produces adrenaline, which is a powerful vasoconstrictor. It raises blood pressure and the blood sugar by increasing the sugar output from the liver. The amount of adrenaline secreted can be increased by excitement, anger, fear, etc.

The reproductive glands

The reproductive glands are different in men and women. In women they are called the ovaries and they produce oestrogen and progesterone. They are responsible for the development of the feminine figure, growth of pubic and axial hair and reproduction. In men they are called the testes and produce testosterone, which is responsible for the changes in voice, increased muscle mass, development of hair on the body and face, reproductive functions and other usual male characteristics. Both sexes produce small amounts of the opposite gender's hormones also.

The pancreas

The pancreas consists of clumps of glands called islets of Langerhans which secrete insulin, which regulates the sugar level in the blood and the conversion of sugar into energy and heat.

The skeletal system

The skeletal system serves two important purposes. One is protecting the softer organs and body tissues, e.g. the skull protects the brain, the ribs protect the lungs and heart, the other is, in concert with the muscles, to provide a means of locomotion or movement e.g. the legs for running, the arms and hands for doing tasks. Erythrocytes and leucocytes and platelets are produced in the bone marrow. (*See* under blood).

The muscular system

The muscular system is responsible for 50% of our weight. The muscles enable us to move both through voluntary action and involuntary action. Voluntary action is when the muscles are under conscious control such as to move a limb, and involuntary action is when things move without us having to think about them, such as in the beating of the heart, or breathing.

The vascular system

The vascular system includes the heart, blood vessels, blood, lymphatic vessels and the lymph.

The heart is the centre of the system, it keeps everything pumping round. It is a muscular organ that rhythmically contracts forcing the blood through the system of vessels. It weighs approximately 255 g. At birth it beats at 130 times a minute, slowing down as we get older to an average of around 70. In an adult during a 24 hour period it pumps 36,000 litres of blood around 20,000 km of blood vessels. It is divided into four sections, one side processes the venous blood while the other deals with the arterial blood. There are two systems of circulation. One is the systemic or general circulation which takes the blood around the body, and the pulmonary circulation which takes the blood to and from the lungs.

The blood vessels which proceed from the heart are called arteries, and they generally carry oxygenated blood (the exception being the pulmonary artery). They are large, hollow and elastic tubes which decrease in diameter as they spread through the body, the smallest being known as capillaries. The blood vessels that take the deoxygenated blood to the heart are known as veins (except for the pulmonary vein.) These are elastic tubes with valves that prevent back flow of the blood. The deoxygenated blood flows from the heart through the pulmonary artery to the lungs, where it is reoxygenated, returned through the pulmonary vein to the heart, and then out to the body via the arteries, returning in the veins to the heart to start all over again.

There are about 5–6 litres of blood in the average adult. Though very complex, it consists of four main components. These are plasma, erythrocytes (red corpuscles), leucocytes (white corpuscles) and platelets. Plasma is the liquid base of blood. It is straw coloured and holds such things as sugar, urea, mineral salts, enzymes and amino acids in solution. Erythrocytes are inert biconcave discs which get their colour from haemoglobin which has the ability to absorb oxygen. Their average life is 120 days. They are produced in the red bone marrow, and first disintegrate in the spleen and then go on to the liver. In a healthy adult there are about 5 million per cubic millimetre of blood, giving around a total of 25 billion per human adult. (End to end they would circle the earth more than four times!) These cells carry the oxygen around the body, and on their return journey bring back waste products, primarily carbon dioxide. Leucocytes or phagocytes are larger than erythrocytes, and are irregular in shape and have a nucleus. They are produced in the bone marrow, and in health number around 8,000 per cubic millimetre. They protect the body against infection and have the power to ingest bacteria. When the body is under attack from infection the leucocytes multiply rapidly. Platelets or thrombocytes average about 250,000 per cubic millimetre of blood. They are derived from large multinucleated cells in the bone marrow. They are essential to the action of coagulation.

The lymphatic system

The lymphatic system is a second circulatory system which is interlinked with the blood circulation. The base material of this system is a liquid called lymph which has been exuded from the capillaries. It nourishes the tissue cells, and carries away waste. This liquid is drained off through Lymph vessels which are joined together forming larger lymph vessels, while conveying the lymph towards the heart. They have valves to prevent back flow like the veins have. On the way to the heart the lymph passes through lymph nodes, which act as filters to help prevent infection from getting into the blood stream and to add lymphocytes. There are about 100 lymphatic nodes around the body, these include the axially glands in the armpit, the inguinals in the groin, the submandibular glands under the lower jaw bone. When there is infection these swell.

The neurological system

The neurological system is divided into two main parts: the central nervous system (cerebrospinal) and the autonomic nervous system (including the sympathetic and parasympathetic). The autonomic nervous system supplies all body structures over which we have no control. All internal organs have a double supply of nerves from this system, the sympathetic nerves have the effect of increasing body activity and to speed it up, while the parasympathetic slows down body activity.

The brain is inside the skull. It is the central command station for actions in the body. The brain is encased in protective membranes called the meninges and cerebrospinal fluid which cushion the brain from banging against the insides of the skull. It weighs around 1360 g and it is estimated that it has twelve billion neurones or nerve cells. It has three main parts: the cerebrum, the medulla oblongata and the cerebellum. The cerebellum contains 70% of the nervous system and consists of the right and left cerebral hemispheres. There are different areas which control various functions, such as the motor cortex which deals with voluntary movement, the sensory cortex which deals with bodily sensations, the frontal lobe that deals with personality, the occipital lobe which deals with sight and the middle of the brain which deals with hearing and speech. There is a medulla oblongata which contains the nerve fibres and joins the cerebellum and cerebrum to the spinal cord. Its functions include automatic and unconscious control of such activities as breathing, heart beat and digestion. The cerebellum's main functions concern muscle coordination and equilibrium of the body. The spinal cord which is a continuation of the medulla oblongata extends through the vertebrae (spine) carrying the messages from 'head office' to the parts of the body.

The digestive system

The digestive system is responsible for processing the food we take into our bodies to make it useable as fuel for energy, heat, growth and repair. The digestive tract or alimentary canal starts at the mouth and ends at the anus, and is over 10 m long. From the mouth where the food begins to be broken down by the saliva, it passes to the pharynx which is a muscular tube with seven openings into it. These are the mouth, oesophagus, larynx, two posterior apertures of the nose and two Eustachian tubes. The food passes from the pharynx into the oesophagus, which is a muscular tube. From here the food goes into the stomach, a muscular sac, which has glands producing gastric juice that contains the enzymes pepsin and rennin, and hydrochloric acid. The food carries on through the small intestine and on into the large intestine, the goodness being absorbed and the waste matter being passed on to eventually be evacuated through the rectum and anus. The digestive system is supported by the liver and the pancreas. The liver is on the right hand side of the body below the diaphragm. It is the largest organ in the body. It measures 25–30 cm across and 15–18 cm from back to front and weighs around 1.5 kg. It has many functions, one of which is the production and storage of bile. It can produce up to 1 litre a day. It is passed to the gall bladder where it is concentrated by eight to ten times and stored until required when it passes into the duodenum which is the first part of the small intestine. Bile contains bile salts, and bile pigments which are derived from the disintegration of red blood cells. The bile salts are reabsorbed and reused, as they promote efficient digestion of fats. The pancreas is a cream coloured gland, 15–20 cm long and about 4 cm wide (*see* diagram on page 159).

The respiratory system

The respiratory system is responsible for taking oxygen into our bodies and discharging carbon dioxide and some water.

There are two parts: the upper and lower respiratory tract. The upper respiratory tract includes the nose, mouth, throat, larynx and sinus cavities in the head. Air is brought in through the nose, where it is filtered and warmed before progressing to the lower respiratory tract which includes the trachea (windpipe), the bronchi and lungs. The lungs are the principal organs of the respiratory system and situated inside the rib cage. They are inert, i.e. they do not work themselves. They are worked by a system using atmospheric pressure created by a muscular wall situated under them, known as the diaphragm. As this muscle contracts and relaxes it creates a change in the volume of the thorax and thereby a change in atmospheric pressure inside the lungs themselves. This causes air to be sucked in and blown out of them, thus inspiration and expiration of air is brought about. The lungs are greyish in colour and spongy looking. They are lined with alveoli, minute air chambers which have very thin walls. In these walls are the capillaries of the pulmonary system. The fresh air is taken in, and it gives off its oxygen to the blood at this point, and then takes on the carbon dioxide from the blood to be expelled in the next breath out. The average adult breaths around 13,650 litres of air a day. The normal rate of breathing is around sixteen times a minute. The respiratory system has the biggest intake of any system in the body, and is also the most important system. We can only survive for a few minutes without air.

The genito-urinary system

The genito-urinary system, the excretory and reproductive systems, often put together because a number of the organs are common to both, includes the ovaries, fallopian tubes, uterus, urethra, ureter and the urinary bladder. The ovaries, fallopian tubes and uterus are found in females only. They are positioned in the pelvic cavity. There are two ovaries, one on the left and one on the right, each is about the size of an almond.

These produce unfertilised eggs, one every 28 days, during the reproductive life. They also produce hormones which influence sex characteristics and control changes in the uterus during the menstrual cycle. The fallopian tubes are about 10 cm long and they are there to transport the egg from the ovaries to the uterus. The uterus is a muscular pear shaped organ, measuring about 7.5 cm long by 5 cm wide and 2.5 cm thick. It is positioned between the bladder at the front and the rectum at the back. The uterus is where the egg, if fertilised, embeds for it to grow. At the lower end of the uterus is the cervix leading into the vagina which is a muscular canal, which connects the above organs to the outside of the body, acting as a birth canal if required. The male genital organs include the testes, of which there are two. They are held in the scrotum, which is a pouch-like organ hanging outside the body, in front of which is the penis, which is used to deliver the sperm to enable fertilisation of the female egg, and to act as a way for urine to leave the body.

The urinary part of this system includes the kidneys. These are approximately 10 cm long and 5 cm wide and 2.5 cm thick. They are positioned against the posterior abdominal wall at the normal waistline, with the right kidney being slightly lower than the left. The function of the kidney is to separate certain waste products from the blood, to help maintain the composition of the blood at a constant level, despite variations in diet and amount of fluid intake. As the blood is passed through the kidneys quantities of water, salts, urea and glucose are filtered into the capsules of Bowman and on into the convoluted tubules. From here all the glucose, most of the water and salts, and some of the urea are returned to the blood vessels. The remainder is passed via the calyces into the kidney pelvis as urine. Around 150–180 litres of fluid are processed by the kidneys per day, but only 1.5 litres of it leaves the body as urine. The ureters are 26–30 cm long, and are fine muscular tubes which carry the urine from the kidney pelvis to the bladder, which is a muscular sac lying behind the pubic bone. The urethra is a narrow muscular tube which takes the urine from the bladder out of the body. In a female this is 4 cm long, and in a male 20 cm long. In the male the urethra is duel purpose in that it carries both the urine and the semen (reproductive fluid). In the male is also passes through the prostate gland which is about the size of a chestnut. Its secretions help to maintain sperm activity.

The Energy Body

We are more than just blood and bones. We have an energy body, which to most people is invisible. Despite this, it should not be discounted as it has a dramatic effect on us. If someone is overpowering you, or you have a shock then you can feel yourself shrinking, and feeling smaller. When someone is ill they often look *shrunken*. If you have a nice surprise then suddenly you feel brighter and taller. This is because the vitality/energy body is being affected and in turn it is having an affect on us physically too. This body changes quicker than the physical, but the two are interrelated and inter-react with each other. What affects one will finally affect the other. So treating the energetic body can bring about a change in the physical. Most poor health starts on an energetic level, but if left untreated it will manifest into physical symptoms. A whole book could be written on this subject alone. Many have been, so the following will only be enough to help explain the theory of auras and chakras used in some Reiki treatments.

The energetics of the body consist of three basic parts:
1 the subtle bodies,
2 the chakras and
3 the nadis.

In Reiki the positions are mainly involved with the chakras, however as Reiki travels around the systems, both physical and energetic, all parts of both systems are affected, whichever you are using.

The subtle bodies

There are four subtle bodies. They surround the physical body in layers forming a human aura, much like the little boy in the hot breakfast cereal advert, with his red glow of warmth.

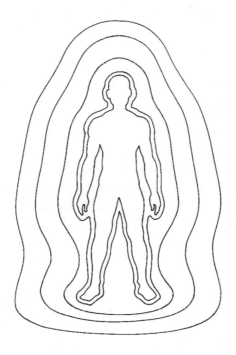

The human aura

The etheric body

The closest to the body is the etheric body which resembles the physical body in shape. It affects the shape of the physical body, the creative energy and vital force, and also physical sensations. It draws energy from the sun via the solar plexus chakra and from the earth via the root chakra. It then stores the energies feeding them through to the physical body via the nadis and chakra systems. We can damage this flow from within ourselves by negative thoughts, stress, poor diet and other self abuse, e.g. nicotine, alcohol, drugs. These weaken this body, and as it affects the physical body, disease results. This can be prevented, as it can be detected in the energetic body in advance of the physical body showing any signs. The ethereal body also acts as a go between, between the physical and the higher vibratory bodies, namely the astral, mental and spiritual bodies.

The astral body

The astral or emotional body occupies the same space as the physical body, and supports the emotions, feelings and character of a person. It is egg -shaped and can extend several yards around the person. This body shows to those that can see it, as a spectacle of ever-changing colours, becoming dark and cloudy if the emotions contain fear, anger, worry, depression, etc. It stores any unresolved issues, fears and feelings which in turn continue to be transmitted through the emotional body, not just affecting the person, but also sending messages to the outside world, often attracting like to like, presenting a mirror of the fears and insecurities etc. and in so doing often confirming those negative states. Of course if positive and happy messages are being sent out then these too will be mirrored, and this perception of the world will be confirmed.

The mental body

The mental body produces our thoughts, ideas and intuitive and rational perceptions. The vibrations of this body are higher than the ethereal and astral bodies, and thus its structure is less dense. It too is egg shaped and as the person progresses to a higher vibration its volume can be equal to both the ethereal and astral bodies combined. It can radiate several yards around the physical body. It inter-reacts with the other two bodies, and if they are not clear and working well due to negative states this can adversely affect its functioning.

The spiritual body

The spiritual body has the highest vibrational frequency of all the bodies. In the case of a spiritually developed person it can extend miles around the physical body in a circle. You may have noticed that when truly spiritual person walks in to the room, the whole atmosphere changes, becoming light and pleasurable to be in.

The chakras

The chakras. There are a recorded 88,000 chakras on the body. Traditionally we use the seven primary chakras when giving a Reiki treatment. These are positioned along the spinal column and are closely related to the endocrine system. Chakras are receptors, transformers and means of transferring energy. They are located in the ethereal body. They are like funnels with petals on, the lower the vibration the less number of petals, i.e. the base chakra only has four petals while the

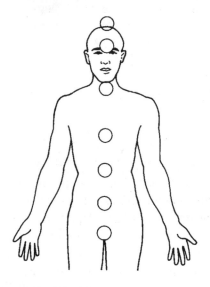

The main chakras

crown chakra has around a thousand. These petals represent the *nadis*, which is a system of channels through which the energies flow. From the centre of each chakra there is a stem which goes to the spine, within which runs an energy channel connecting each chakra with it and with each other. Each chakra has a front and a back. The word 'chakra' is Sanskrit for 'wheel', and the chakras are continuously spinning, taking in or giving off energy depending upon the direction in which they are rotating, and the sex of the person. The directions being reversed for each gender, and alternating for each chakra. If the chakras become blocked or out of sync then this affects both the energetic bodies and the physical. Reiki can help to clear and rebalance them.

There are many associations connected with the chakras including colours, elements, symbols, body parts and glands, astrological signs, gems stones, essential oils to name but a few. Here are a few thoughts on each of the seven, that could be helpful when used with Reiki. I would just mention that each person can experience each chakra in a very personal way, and so to get your own interpretation you could sit quietly and *feel* into it, and see what *you* come up with, you might even *see* it.

The base chakra

The position of the base chakra is at the base of the spine pointing downwards. Its colour is red, and it is associated with the element of Earth. It is symbolised by a lotus with four petals. It governs the following body parts: bones, teeth, nails, the spinal column, the anus, rectum, colon, prostate gland, blood and cell building. It is associated with the adrenal glands. It gives us a connection to Earth, and is the foundation for the other higher chakras, it is also mutually connected with the crown chakra. This chakra is about survival and procreation. If this chakra is blocked you may well be low in both physical and emotional energy.

The sacral chakra

This chakra is situated above the pubic bone and below the tummy button. Its colour is orange, and its element is water. It is symbolised by a six-petalled lotus. It is the chakra of health and pleasure and immunity from disease. It is related to the following physical parts: the pelvic girdle, reproductive organs, kidneys, bladder along with the body liquids, i.e. blood, lymph, gastric juices and semen. It is associated with the gonads, namely the ovaries, prostate gland, and testicles. This chakra is related to the sexual energies and creativity, being connected to the element of water from which all life is thought to have come. Our relationships, especially with those of the opposite sex are influenced by this centre. Imbalances in this chakra can manifest in conditions which affect the sexual body parts, such as ovarian cysts, lumps in the breasts, cervical cancer, prostate problems, impotence.

The solar plexus chakra

The solar plexus chakra, is situated above the navel and at the base of the ribs. Its colour is yellow and is associated with the element of fire. It is symbolised by a ten-petalled lotus. This is the chakra that takes power from the sun, and passes it on to the other chakras to keep them healthy. It gives us both spiritual and physical energy. It is related to the following body parts: lower back, abdomen, digestive system, stomach, liver, spleen, gallbladder and the autonomic nervous system. It is associated with the pancreas. This centre helps us to perceive other's vibrations, and in turn it also projects ours for others to *see* or react to. Being out of balance in this chakra creates a desire to be constantly active and proving yourself, and a feeling of unrest within.

The heart chakra

The heart chakra is positioned over the heart. Its colour is green, or sometimes pink and gold. Its element is air. It is symbolised by a twelve-petalled lotus. It is associated with the following body parts: heart, upper back, the lower part of the lungs, the blood and circulation and the skin. The gland it is related to is the thymus, which helps in stimulating and strengthening the immune system. This is the central chakra and creates a bridge between the lower vibrating chakras that are closely related to the physical to those with higher vibrations that are more spiritual in nature. This chakra is about unconditional love, connection, acceptance, transformation, powerful healing. If it is not functioning well you may feel uncomfortable with soft emotions, and find it hard to accept from others.

The throat chakra

The throat chakra is positioned at the throat. Its colour is pale blue or silver. Its element is ether. It is symbolised by a 16-petalled lotus. It is associated with the neck, throat and jaw, ears, voice, trachea, bronchial tubes, upper lungs, oesophagus and arms. The gland that is related to it is the thyroid, which plays an important part in growth, regulation of calcium levels, and the speed of the transformation of food into energy. As you might expect this centre is about creativity, self-expression and communication. Malperformance of this chakra can result in poor communication within yourself, i.e. between the body and mind, this can manifest in thoughtless actions. Stutters may also appear, and expression may become coarse, cool or blatant. A fear of expressing yourself may also result.

The third eye or brow chakra

The third eye or brow chakra is situated between the eye brows at the top of the nose. Its colour is violet and it is symbolised by a 96-petalled lotus. It is associated with the face, eyes, ears, nose, sinuses, cerebellum and central nervous system. The gland related to it is the pituitary, which is the master gland, regulating all the other glands in the endocrine system. This centre is the one of intuition, psychic awareness and higher mental powers, our memory. This is where our thoughts can manifest matter, where we can make changes to our outer world through our minds. When this chakra is not harmonious it will give a feeling of being top heavy, with to much emphasis on the mental stuff, reason and intellect everything being filtered through the rational mind. It may also bring about a state of confusion.

The crown chakra

The crown chakra is situated on the top, at the centre of the head. Its colours are violet, indigo, white and gold. It is symbolised by a 1000-petalled lotus. It is associated with the cerebrum and the pineal gland. This chakra is the highest vibration of the seven, it can represent the highest human perfection, it is where our essence is. We connect here with the cosmic rays, and of course Reiki. With this chakra you can become at one with all. If we do not have this centre open, then we may well feel unconnected and separated, and experience feelings of fear. Taking time with nature and beautiful things enhances the development of this chakra.

Again I stress that this is a very brief dip into the wonderful world of our energy bodies, and as such it cannot hope to offer a truly balanced portrayal of them.

Personal Insights

Illnesses

From Jennie Austin . . .

Depression

A lady came to me having been diagnosed as having clinical depression. She was signed off work, and the doctor wanted her to have some pills, which she did not favour. Previously she had come to me, just to try out Reiki. She had seen it mentioned somewhere and so just came out of interest. She had found it very relaxing, and said she would return in the future. However I did not hear from her again until she phoned asking if I thought Reiki could help her present problem.

When she arrived she was far from the enthusiastic person that I had met previously. She was slouched, and looking uncared for. Her normally bright appearance was not apparent at all.

She came for weekly treatments for about ten weeks, missing a couple along the way, as she took a holiday. During this time she experienced quite a lot of emotional swings, some of which we could identify with past events, some of which we never did find a cause for them. The wonderful thing with Reiki is that you don't always need to know what caused the problem, you just need to be willing to let go of it. This she did, and when I last saw her she was bright, smart and full of enthusiasm for life, having started a new job, and making plans to do some retraining.

Frozen shoulder

I had a lady coming for aromatherapy, who had a frozen shoulder. She had fallen one day and it had not been the same since. She had five massages with appropriate essential oil mixes, but although she enjoyed the treatments and they eased the discomfort, the mobility of the shoulder did not improve. I suggested that she might like to try a complete Reiki session, or to be more exact a series of four on following days. She was eager to try anything as this shoulder was distressing her.

When she arrived on the third day, she was excitedly flailing her arm around like a windmill. The shoulder's range of movement had improved markedly. After the fourth treatment the shoulder was completely free. One happy person became a fully paid up member of the Reiki Fan Club! She still comes for relaxation treatments, and is thinking of taking the First-Degree training.

Asthma

Alice developed asthma. She had to use a puffer lots of times a day in order that she could breath at all. She was not happy taking the drugs in the inhaler, so she decided to use Reiki to try and ease the breathing. We met for six consecutive days, and she received treatments lasting from 90 to 40 minutes, getting shorter as the days progressed. There was a noticeable difference in the form that Reiki took, as her needs changed from day to day. It was scorching hot, warm and even cool, and the intensity started out by being very strong, but became softer as the days passed. She was able to reduce the number of times that she needed to use the inhaler, and now only uses it on rare occasions. She supported herself throughout with Reiki self-treatments, and of course continues to do so.

Alleviating symptoms caused by leukaemia

Jo came for aromatherapy massage, as she had heard that some specific oils could help leukaemia, and anyway massage would help as part of her dedicated health care programme. She was in her sixties and had been a nurse. I'm not sure how we changed from aromatherapy to Reiki, but we did. She decided to train in Reiki (she is now a Master) Along with an informed (and delicious) nutritional regime and Reiki, including diligent self-treatment, her blood count is now practically normal. She is healthier than many who don't have a health problem and leads an active life.

Lack of energy

A lady in her fifties rang me. She sounded as though she had hardly enough energy to talk. I knew that in the past six to nine months of her life there had been a series of disasters and poor health, and she sounded as though she had had enough. She wanted me to help, but to be honest I was almost at a loss as to where to start there was so much wrong. I suggested that if she would like Reiki, then I would be happy to help her, as that way everything would be taken into the picture and treated the best way. She agreed and arrived the next day, struggling up the stairs, looking a wreck. She collapsed onto the treatment couch, and just lay. After I had finished the treatment, which was like a sponge soaking up water, she slithered off, and left with a suggestion from me to go home and rest to let the Reiki do its best. I saw her three days later, looking smart and bursting with energy. I wasn't too surprised and as I think her main problem stemmed from complete exhaustion. I asked if she had had a good rest when she got home. Her reply was 'No, I stripped the bathroom and wallpapered it!' By the time she had got home she was bursting with vitality.

From Dorothy Berry-Lound . . .
Eczema

Janet, in her early 30s, asked me to look at her hand where her eczema had flared up. Her eczema had largely gone since I found she had an allergy to oranges, and that she had been drinking orange juice every morning, so this flare up was a disappointment to her. Whilst giving Reiki I had got the impression of her moving pieces of paper. I asked her about it and it transpired her husband is a printer. Over the previous week she had been helping him collate papers, not something she did very often. This appeared to be a reaction to the ink. I suggested she wore gloves when she helped him out – it seems to be working!

Back pain

Reg, in his early sixties, was suffering from severe back pain. Unable to move from his summer caravan other than to be taken to the chiropractor, his wife had left him there to come home to do some washing. She rang to see if I could send some distance healing. She said that although Reg didn't know she had asked, it would be okay as he always enjoyed his Reiki treatments with me. I sat down at 10.15 pm with a photo of him and focused all my attention on him for the next 20 minutes, imagining my hands on his lower back. His wife returned to the caravan the next day, and rang me in great excitement to say he had been watching News at Ten and plucked up enough courage to face the pain and get up to go to bed, only to find there was very little pain, in fact it had settled in his hip joints, and he could move quite freely. In the second treatment I concentrated on his hips and he rang to report the pain had moved to his knees. After a course of four distance treatments he reported that he felt better than he had done for years.

From Alice Walkingshaw . . .

Physical pain and stress

The following is a case of someone who improved quite substantially, both mentally, emotionally and physically.

Karen was in her early 40s and complained of intermittent

shooting pains in the right shoulder (she fell on it when a child), pain and stiffness in her neck and chronic tension in her shoulders. She held quite a high managerial position and her job carried a great deal of responsibility with a very heavy workload. She had been signed off work for several months as a result of stress from overwork and had received a course of physiotherapy. Although Karen recognised that her self-esteem was still pretty low, she had recently returned to work (two days a week) hoping to gradually build up to full-time again.

Karen had three one-hour treatments, each a week apart, covering the whole body, with special attention paid (time-wise) to the affected physical areas. When I had tried to mention possible reactions that might be experienced as a result of a Reiki treatment, she had stopped me, saying that she didn't want any ideas put in her head, but rather wanted to remain objective and would let me know if she noticed anything.

At the second session she reported that after the first treatment everything felt really easy for the rest of the day. She had experienced diarrhoea, which started in the middle of the first night and continued for three days. She had been sweating profusely during the night and an odd thing she had noticed was that her urine had been like 'peaty water' and smelled really strong. She had also felt thirsty and drank a lot of water. I assured her that her reactions were normal and were the result of a detoxification process. I noticed her skin colour had improved. She mentioned that on one of her non-working days during the week she had felt absolutely euphoric. She had been feeling more confident, had started wearing her good clothes and jewellery to work, and was receiving and – more significantly – accepting compliments from colleagues. She felt she had made a big step forward.

For the third session I did the same pattern of treatment as for previous sessions, although she said that there were no areas requiring special attention this time. Karen reported that her physical symptoms had eased off and she felt more relaxed in general. She stated that on one particular evening every part of her body had felt sore including her scalp – not really like a normal pain or ache – and this continued into the night. She later realised that since that day she had not noticed any further muscular tension in her shoulders. She had experienced three nightmares all in one night, but none since. I mentioned that I thought her skin now looked as if it was glowing and she agreed. When applying her usual foundation make-up one morning she realised that it no longer matched her skin tone properly and had to go and buy some new stuff.

Improving quality of life

Although this person died shortly after the course of distance healing was begun, I believe that his quality of life was improved and his spirits lifted during his last days thanks to Reiki. Having met him several times over the years, I am of the opinion that he was probably someone who would not normally seek unorthodox methods of treatment for an illness.

The recipient was male, early seventies, suffering from cancer of the gullet. I learned after his death that the cancer had also spread to other internal organs.

Comfort during chronic illness

Shortly after I had been initiated into Reiki II, I received a call one night from Charlie, a friend of my mother, who wondered if Reiki might be able to help him. I explained that although I would not be able to see him in person, I could direct Reiki to him even though he lived about 100 miles away. We agreed that I should begin treating him right away (about 30 minutes each night). I also did some short treatments during the day when it was convenient for me to do so.

Four days later an excited Charlie rang me to say that during the last two days he had been able to eat normally again at every meal. He explained that he had lost 30 lbs in weight over the past two months because he had been unable to keep his food down. He was really keen to continue the treatments. A few days later I learned from my mother that his operation had not gone well and that he had died shortly afterwards. I continued to direct Reiki to Charlie for a number of days to help him in his transition to the next world.

Indigestion

The next is a case of Reiki 'first aid' concerning my husband Dave who developed a disagreement with a takeaway pizza! The outcome converted him from a sceptic to someone who now asks for Reiki if he is significantly unwell or in pain.

I awoke in the middle of the night to hear my Dave saying that he was feeling very sick indeed. He said he was very nauseous and thought he might vomit at any minute. I sat up and placed my hands on his head whereupon his breathing calmed considerably. He then asked for a drink of water which I fetched (remembering to channel Reiki into the water). As it turned out he only managed one sip as the slightest movement made him worse. I got into bed and just lay beside him channelling Reiki through my left hand which I lay over his right hand and told him that the Reiki would still go where it was needed. (I felt that lying quietly was the best thing to do in the circumstances.) I eventually fell asleep. In the morning Dave told me quite emphatically that the Reiki had really helped. He had felt terrible until I put my hands on his head, whereupon he began to feel better. However, when I went to get the water he got worse again. But when I lay down and placed my hand on his, the improvement continued until he fell asleep.

Aches and pains

I would like to tell you of my mother's first experience of Reiki.

My mother (aged 73) is fairly active for her age and likes

gardening. However, one day when visiting me she spent the best part of ten hours working in my garden, barely stopping for food or rest. She loves my garden because it is a challenge. (I do very little in it!) She was very tired when she finally called it a day, saying she had overdone it and would no doubt pay for her over-enthusiasm in aches and pains the next day. In view of this she agreed to a Reiki treatment before bed. She received a whole-body treatment lasting 80 minutes, sleeping through most of it. The next day she was in excellent form and delighted to find she had none of the expected symptoms of over-exertion.

Minor first aid

As someone who has always bruised easily, I am impressed with Reiki's ability to quickly stop bleeding and swelling. I have banged my shin thoroughly a couple of times and my elbow and arm. I find that if Reiki is applied immediately and a hand kept over the area for five to ten minutes, depending on the severity of the situation, there is no bruising or only a redness which disappears leaving no bruise. The same applies to small cuts, which stop bleeding quickly and minor burns which cease hurting and disappear within about half an hour. The best results come from acting immediately, before the body's reaction takes hold. I have also noticed that sometimes, for a short while, the level of pain increases beyond what I would normally expect to experience, while my hand is over the affected area.

From June Woods . . .
Heart attack and complications

A friend of seven years was rushed into hospital, with a possible heart attack, thyroid disorder and other complications. I visited and immediately went to Eve's feet and channelled the Reiki energy through, as the feet contain a map of the body. She really felt the upsurge around the heart and throat areas.

Practising Reiki

Three days running I visited and managed to do her feet, down the left and right sides of her body and also around her throat. Her heart had been exhibiting strange rhythms and we could see this on the monitor to which she was linked. Each day saw a gradual improvement, and when she could return home, I suggested she might stay with me for a few weeks, as I had a bungalow, and therefore no stairs. This we arranged. Her own doctor, and a colleague of mine who is a doctor and also runs a Holistic Alternative Therapy Practice with several other therapists totally supported my decision to care for Eve at home.

Gradually, each day, Eve began to eat a little more and sleep less, and, as the doctor got her medication adjusted, the heartbeat and thyroid became balanced. Each day for this first month Eve had a full Reiki treatment, then I started to just channel the energy through her feet again, so she had a peaceful night's sleep.

Eve is a lady of 77, lively and very interested in many subjects and good to talk with. If she has felt low, I have always been ready to go and give her a top up.

Stroke

One Sunday morning early in November 1996, I had a phone call from my friend Veronica. She asked could I please go round as she felt she'd had a stroke. As she only lived half-a-mile away, I managed to get to her house in fifteen minutes. When I arrived she was walking around as she was afraid of having a thrombosis, having had one several years previously. She got into the bed and I just channelled energy up through the feet, then used some Aura Soma Rescue Oil all down her left side, feeling the Reiki energy follow down the side of the head, neck, arm, side, legs and feet. I put more into the soles of the feet. Panic over, she felt a bit better so I made her a hot drink and she had a sleep. We phoned the doctor who said to go into hospital for a check up. This she did for about four days. I continued with Reiki sessions both in hospital and on her return home.

Back pain

Veronica has been initiated to Reiki I, and offers the energy to people in need. She came to Reiki first after she had phoned me after I had treated her for back pain. She had been on pain killers for about eight years, and she was feeling really sick with pain as their effects wore off. She could not believe that the Reiki had removed the back pain, for three days but then, as she said, she stupidly lifted heavy paving slabs while building a pond! So now she tries to remember to take a break, a doze and not to push herself over the limit. Her dog also loves Reiki, and makes a real fuss of me when I visit.

Overcoming disabling illness

It is very interesting how Linda came to train in Reiki last year. Another initiate, John, who has a lovely hotel in Perthshire, attended a residential Reiki II workshop in February 1996, at a good friend's venue, deep in the hills not far from Loch Ness. This really emphasised his confidence and healing abilities, so much so that when, for the fourth day running, he saw this young woman in a wheelchair, being pushed by her husband and accompanied by a large dog, he stopped his car and introduced himself, feeling it was no coincidence that he had come upon them. In the event he explained that he was a healing channel and offered Linda a session. This turned into three or four more as the couple were having a break in their caravan, not far from John's hotel. The result of these sessions was such a benefit that John phoned me and explained the situation and said he'd suggested that Linda be trained herself.

Linda and I spoke and I immediately warmed to her soft Scottish accent and, as I had the following weekend free, she arranged to come over. They stayed with my friend Veronica, while her brother looked after Rocky the dog. I had the two of them working with each other. Linda is a natural. She does not need her wheelchair now. She went through a period of total excitement and overloading with patients, and she rang and said her legs were playing up and were quite sore. So I said 'The first rule is to nurture yourself, and remember you're not superhuman, and to feel OK about saying no.' She is really creative on her computer and artwork, and as I write will be doing the Reiki II this coming weekend.

From Keith Harris . . .
Aura photography to show illness
My partner, Clarissa, and I first met Jennie one sunny September afternoon at her centre in Inverness. Although we had spoken on the phone and received distance healing and plenty of information from her, nothing could have quite prepared us for our first experience of hands-on Reiki. We had travelled to Scotland as the latest phase in a sustained campaign investigating complementary therapies that might help me combat the rather adverse brain tumour diagnosis I'd received the previous summer. The combination of Jennie's multiple talents in such therapies and a short break in a frequent childhood holiday destination of mine proved irresistible for me, so I was delighted when we could at last travel 'North of the Border'.

Clarissa and I were not alone in attending the centre that afternoon as some of Jennie's Reiki initiates also soon arrived and, most significantly, an aura photographer who had also travelled with his wife from England to Inverness. A plan emerged that would involve 'before and after' aura photos being taken of us, so that any changes in our auras that resulted from the Reiki session might be measured. Using the Polaroid-style camera specially adapted to superimpose an impression of our auric fields gained from an electrical measurement of different points on our palms, he took the before shots of us and explained what he could tell from the practically instant results. In my case, there was a predominantly green hue surrounding my head, but with a substantial bit *missing* over my right shoulder.

The photographer described this as the clearest example of a 'personal loss' that he had seen in such a shot, and suggested that I must have recently experienced some considerable sadness in my life. Given that he had absolutely no knowledge of my background, Clarissa, Jennie and I were each amazed at this, as immediately we each thought of my mother, who had passed away less than two years before, and with whom I had a very close relationship. This photograph became important therefore as the first tangible evidence of how the loss of my mother had affected me. The appearance of the green colour apparently signified that I was receiving healing (which was a good sign), but that 'one or two more colours in there would signify a healthier state of affairs'. Clarissa's first photo was also in need of more colours, to alter its mainly red content which reflected the emotional strain she had been under recently.

The Reiki session started, with subdued light, subtle music and an atmosphere of such benign intent, it was difficult not to be moved emotionally. Jennie and one of her students, Maureen, were working on me, whilst the others treated Clarissa. Soon I found myself drifting from the treatment table on which I was lying to some delightful intermediate place on the borders of consciousness and slumber, aware of the symmetrical hand positions being adopted on my body, yet abdicating any responsibility for my wellbeing as I relaxed totally in the warmth of the care and attention that was being devoted to me.

All too soon three-quarters of an hour had elapsed and I found myself being very gently brought back to reality, despite the resistance of my exceptionally comfortable body! After a few minutes of essential recovery from the pampered state we were in, the aura photographer returned, and Clarissa and I were photographed again. He was pleased that the equipment he was using had detected a change in the red area surrounding Clarissa, with an orange area suggesting progress from the earlier picture as a result of the Reiki healing she too had enjoyed.

When my 'after' photo appeared, however, my head was surrounded by virtually all the colours of the rainbow! All of us were surprised and delighted at the same time at this total transformation from the mainly green appearance of my 'before' photo, with even the 'hole in my aura layer' being no longer visible. Apparently it was the most obvious measurement of the effect that Reiki can have which anyone there had ever seen. When we emerged into the still-bright autumn sunshine a little later, it took Clarissa and I some time to acclimatise ourselves to our surroundings, and not because it was a different country. Where we had 'been' through the experience of Reiki had made the world seem a better place, and we were just so thrilled at being introduced to just a little of the power that is around us that can be channelled for healing.

[*Author's note*: Keith and Clarissa went on to be initiated to the First Degree.]

Using Reiki First-Degree teaching

Going from sleeping with my right hand cradling the side of my head, to trying to tap into the forces which bind the universe together might seem a bit of a leap but, essentially, my simplest form of Reiki (self)-treatment makes just that jump. It's been a comforting and relaxing way to use the Reiki First-Degree teaching that I received from Jennie, yet it is, I firmly believe, every bit as helpful to me as more extensive self-healing sessions. I particularly like the way in which it seems to generate warmth, encourage positive thoughts and help me get off to sleep all at the same time! But much more than that, I can feel the good that regular use of the technique can do.

By just aiming to channel healing energy into the side of my head where the site of my 1996 biopsy lies (which revealed the second-trickiest kind of brain tumour), I feel that even this most straightforward use of Reiki has contributed to my continuing apparent success in combating that diagnosis.

The months of research into complementary therapies that followed this news made me aware of a huge variety of approaches to healing. A comprehensive 'A to Z' of such therapies would present a baffling array of options that would undoubtedly leave a patient confused and exhausted (and broke!) if each of them were experienced around the same time. Instead, the generally accepted advice is to try just a few different complementary therapies so that their individual merits can be measured, and favourites selected. One attraction of these therapies is their diversity and limited 'quantities' of therapies in numerical terms can be more than compensated for by their individual 'qualities', provided patients genuinely feel happy with the choices they have made.

It cannot, of course, be stated often enough that a significant part of the power of complementary therapies lies in this very choice that they offer patients, enabling people who are otherwise 'examined', 'treated' or 'operated upon' to take more active responsibility for their own recovery, and letting them use their own initiative to help themselves to get better, alongside the available 'orthodox' options. Through the research I was able to do, I chose a range of therapies based on my growing understanding of the power of so-called 'vibrational therapies', and as each of them shared generally similar principles, I felt confident that they would be 'complementary' not only to the orthodox treatment I was receiving, but also to each other.

Although different people will prefer different approaches, and rightly so, the particular combination which follows works for me! First, having a career in music education for fifteen years, I had no difficulty in understanding the therapeutic effect of music, but in particular I discovered more about the power of African drumming during an idyllic weekend spent with Clarissa in darkest . . . Somerset! Also in Somerset, I had my voice analysed and I received tailor-made 'Signature Sounds' with specific healing frequencies. Next, we attended sessions with a colour therapist who also uses crystal and other healing therapies. Previously I referred to having my aura revealingly photographed (before and after Reiki healing). I regularly receive distance healing from Jennie. I also attended a Matthew Manning Healing Circle and now attend one-to-one sessions with him. I visit Harry Oldfield, who not only takes illuminating 'PIP' scans, but also treats me with electro-crystal therapy.

It would take numerous books to do justice to all of these vibrational therapies, but to help, you will find a few titles listed at the end of this book, which have helped me both to understand the links between them and build up my overall strategy. Suffice to say in the space available that the different kinds of vibrations connected with each of these diverse techniques attempt to employ, amongst other things – a principle which is related to music itself. Just as we are all made up of vibrating particles (as physicists tell us) as opposed to solid, still matter, and lack of harmony within us should be potentially correctable through exposure to the resonating influence of harmonic vibrations which have no 'imbalance' or 'dis-ease'. A good analogy might be the enthusiastic participation in 'Auld Lang Syne' at Hogmanay by someone with even the most uncertain voice when surrounded by experienced, 'in-tune' singers heartily lending support! It's a great principle for someone who's worked in music to employ when striving for health, and I for one can well believe that vibrational therapies, Reiki amongst them, have been tipped to become the medicine of the twenty-first century.

From Steve Austin . . .
Warts

For a few years now I have been getting warts on my hands and fingers and have had to have regular sessions at the doctor's to get them burnt off, using liquid nitrogen. In fact, as I left one appointment I would book for the next session which would be in about one month's time – just right to catch the next crop! Then I discovered Reiki. After a while I thought, 'I'll try this on my warts.' So I began by concentrating on one only, holding or covering with my other hand as best I could for several minutes, several times a day, for a few weeks. This can be done at any time, when sitting reading, or watching the TV or walking etc. The wart then began to dry up and started to shrink and within a couple of months had totally gone. Of course, a soon as I had seen the first one start to dry up, then I started on others, and they too disappeared. At present I only have two tiny ones which are fading. Wart a carry on. (Sorry!)

From Phyl Parsons . . .
Ankle pain

I suddenly developed a very painful heel and ankle, so I asked my daughter-in-law, Dorothy, for some distance Reiki. The pain went as quickly as it had come and, in talking to Dorothy, discovered that the pain was connected to my big toe (I had an operation on my toe the previous year). Thinking back I realised that in using my sewing machine I had been favouring the front of my foot and putting pressure on the heel. Reiki had cured again.

From Senga Hodgson . . .
Arthritis; depression

Heidi was manic depressive from the age of 17, and was prescribed DF118 which made her feel very mellow, almost drunk. At the age of 19 she took herself off the medication, and from time to time she still has bouts of depression. At the age of 20 she was diagnosed as having arthritis in her thoracic vertebrae and in her legs but it is thought that it had started either at birth or around five years of age. It used to be only her legs that were painful, but in the last year her back has become just as painful, if anything worse than her legs, and the pain continued to worsen.

I used Heidi as a case study for my Reiki I training. Heidi hoped for help to ease the pain in her back and legs, and so we decided to do Reiki treatments four days in a row, for about an hour each time. On the first session her head, neck and shoulders felt very warm, but at the same time her arms and hands felt a dead weight. When I moved onto the sixth position across her stomach she felt the strangest of experiences, which Heidi herself explained as a fast whizzing, then an explosion going out of her body through her stomach. Her eyes sprung open and she felt quite startled by it. Her legs felt warm and again very heavy, almost like the circulation had been cut off, and her feet were freezing. She said she felt very relaxed and at peace. Near the end her head began thumping and she experienced rushing impulses through her legs. When my hands were on her buttock area she felt that there was somebody else there running their fingers up and down her legs. Whilst I was giving the treatment I felt very cold. I felt my hands very tingly on a lot of occasions.

On the second treatment Heidi reported that her legs had become very painful the previous evening after having the Reiki. She had taken some painkillers and fallen asleep only to wake up to her back being extremely sore. During the treatment her head was again warm, and when I moved to the sixth position over her abdomen her back started to become very painful, but very warm. The pain shifted and the area still felt warm once I had moved on, then it died down. She felt very relaxed and calm during and after the treatment. As soon as I had started the treatment I felt tremendous heat coming through my hands. When I reached the abdomen my hands felt warm, and then they started to tingle like pins and needles, this lasted for the five minutes I was in this position. I felt the same while my hands were on her buttocks. This time I felt warm while giving the treatment.

The third treatment – Heidi felt very calm throughout the treatment. She felt very intense heat at the sixth position, and her lower back became painful, but this eased off after a while. I felt very warm throughout the whole treatment. My hands felt very hot and prickly on the first and sixth positions.

The fourth treatment – Heidi felt her head and face very warm at the beginning of the treatment, and again intense heat at the sixth position, but this time her back was not painful. She felt very peaceful and relaxed during and afterwards. My hands had felt hot at the beginning of the treatment and again at the sixth position.

Conclusion. Since the beginning of the treatment Heidi's legs have improved in that the stiffness has lessened, and her emotional state for the time being is stable.

This is a good example of how tangible the movement of energy can be. We are generally not aware of it, but Reiki reawakens our finer sensitivity.

From Violet Cochrane . . .
Emotional problems
One girl who came to me was having emotional problems. She had had Reiki before and responded to the relaxation of Reiki wonderfully well. A few days later she came to the door with a lovely bouquet, and she looked beautiful. She said that when I held her hand during the session she had felt she understood what everything was about, the love that flowed through from the Reiki taught her what she needed to know. She did not have to come back.

Practising Reiki

Trust the insight Reiki gives you

Another lass came twice for Reiki, then phoned and asked to come for spiritual healing, which she did, and that really affected her. She then phoned to see if she could come for instruction in spiritual healing. I chatted to her for an evening and directed her to the Healing Centre.

You have never seen such a change in a girl (woman!). You see the Reiki knew what she needed at this particular time.

Joint strain

The first time I gave Reiki to Valerie my daughter she was suffering from tennis elbow. Afterwards she said she had never experienced such a loving energy. Her arm was much better after the Reiki and she was able to go and do some really heavy gardening work.

Leg pain

My husband who couldn't walk without dreadful pain in his legs, found that after regular Reiki his legs were free of pain and still are after two years.

Alleviating the symptoms of ME

A school teacher who had been off work for six months with ME came willingly as one of my subjects and had Reiki as often as she could, as she wanted to get back to teaching when the school resumed in six weeks. The first thing she felt was the relaxation from Reiki and the nightmares she had been suffering went away. Two or three sessions a week led to her getting back to work, part-time and she has continued so. The ME had been bad for a few years and she had been off work a lot, so it meant a great deal to get back.

From Claire Winchester
A symbol to help disturbed energy fields

In the process of receiving a healing attunement, one of my clients, who wishes to be known simply as AC, saw the image of a symbol. He drew it out for me afterwards and we both shook our heads over it, not knowing what it meant. A short while later, I felt an intuitive urge to go into a local newsagents where a health magazine caught my eye. Returning home, a leaflet fell out of the magazine, advertising a mail order book company. Perusing the leaflet I noticed a Reiki book whose publication I had been eagerly awaiting. When the book arrived a week later on leafing through it, I found at the back, the symbol as seen by AC. As you can imagine, I was on the phone right away – 'Guess what? I've found your symbol, what its name is and what it is for'. Now AC had been experiencing problems with disturbed energy fields in the old house in which he was staying. All the efforts to calm, to balance, to remove the energies up to then had been fruitless. The feeling of unrest, the noises, bangs and crashes in the night had persisted. We had not been addressing this problem in the healing attunement, but somehow the Reiki *knew* that help was needed in this field and sent an appropriate symbol. It was called *Kyo ko* and was for the removal of unwanted energies and spirits. AC went to work drawing out the symbol in the air, especially into the corners of the room. He could feel the negative energies departing and at first registered a hollow feeling left behind, until he remembered my suggestion to fill any spaces left with positive feeling and light. Needless to say the unrest and disruptions have never returned and one of the health problems at the physical level cleared up simultaneously!

From Anna Baker . . .
ME, fatigue and depression

'Reiki will find you when you are ready for it.'

This was certainly true for me. Reiki came into my life six

months into a personal flirtation with ME and depression, and though the cycle which changed my life dramatically had already begun, Reiki marked for me a turning point in my apathy and self retribution.

'Reiki is a tool for change'

With the onset of the fatigue some time during the autumn term of my second year at university, came a fleeting intuition that my illness had a greater significance at that time in my life than the mere convenience of not being able to attend my lectures or make my deadlines.

A growing sense of unease began to open my heart to the possible meaning of this illness. My body was protesting at my university attendance. Did this mean that I had made a wrong decision in my life? But I was enjoying my lectures, enjoying experimenting with my new command of the Russian language. Moreover, if I was not in the right place, then what should I be doing? I had no idea.

Fatigue led to depression and confusion. So many questions, so little enthusiasm to answer them. Why am I unfulfilled here? Where should my life go? What other skills could I possibly have?

My response was simply to shut down and hide in the safety of my duvet. Sometime in the New Year I gave into my longings for home, for the West Country. Being ill and stuck in Newcastle, family seemed a million miles away. Finally in returning to my roots, a doorway opened that would lead me to a whole new journey.

I took my first positive steps toward self-healing, it was here that I first learned about Reiki. From a handful of cards and leaflets that I gathered from the local crystal shop, one stuck out above the rest. It was a small card simply inscribed with the word 'Reiki' and the name of the practitioner. I have not looked back since.

After one treatment, I felt the apathy slip away. I felt space to re-energise, take stock and a readiness to heal myself.

After four treatments I knew that I wanted to learn Reiki for myself.

It is now two years since that illness and I now listen very carefully to what my body tells me and act much sooner when I sense an adjustment is needed in my life. I am now fit and healthy and often ride my bicycle to work. A long way from the days when I could not get out of bed even to feed myself. But more importantly I have found my way back to my spiritual path in life and am now engaged in work, which truly fits with my life purpose.

From Catherine Palombo . . .
Stress attack

While in the homeopathic hospital I had a stress attack with rapid heart beat. I got up at 3am and told two sisters and a nurse, how I felt, but they just said 'It must be the remedy, it's working on you' and did nothing more to ease what was happening to me at that moment. I went back to bed, still feeling dreadful, hoping that soon they would come along to see how I was. In the meantime I sat upright in bed and did a Reiki healing on myself. Next thing I knew was the lights going on in the ward, and it was getting up time. I must have slept sound. Thanks to Reiki.

Personal Experiences of Reiki

From Jennie Austin . . .
Reiki can keep you warm!

One night when I was staying in a B & B, I realised as I crawled into bed, pleasantly tired, that I had forgotten to fill my hot water bottle. As the owners had kindly given up their room for me, and were sleeping in the living room, through which I would go to get to the kitchen, and the kettle, I realised that I would have to get warm in some other way. I piled my coat and dressing gown on top of the duvet, put on socks and a jumper, but still I felt cold. Getting more miserable by the moment, and anticipating a night of sleeplessness, I started to do my nightly Reiki self-treatment. Of course! Why hadn't I thought of it myself. Reiki helps where it is needed. Soon I was as warm as toast, and had a wonderful night's sleep.

Reiki and crystals

Before I had been initiated to the Second Degree, I was asked to help a friend's daughter, who lived many miles away. Although I could send a form of distance healing I really felt that she would benefit from the Reiki. I wracked my brains to think of a way, or to find a Reiki contact nearer to her. All to no avail. I sat quietly for a moment or two and asked for the answer. Then the thought popped into my mind to Reiki a crystal and send that. Crystals are wonderful. They are programmable (see how we use them in so many appliances these days). I sat with the crystal in my hands for a while, then sent it to her, for her to carry with her. She says it helped her no end.

Feelings of panic and helplessness

I went to outpatients, for what might be called a non-invasive procedure, i.e. an MRI scan. This is used to take pictures of the insides of the body. My specialist had told me that it was just like putting your head into a washing machine. 'Fine, ' I thought, 'no problem there.' Being a fairly well-disciplined and easy-going person I did not envisage there being any hitches. I had my instructions, i.e. no eye make-up, no metal clasps, zips, buttons, buckles or jewellery and do not take any plastic cards with magnetic strips into the room. No problem! How wrong can you be?

I was asked to lie on a trolley-type thing, and have my head secured with straps to keep it still for the 'photos' to be taken. Then they pushed me back into the 'washing machine'. The only catch was that it wasn't quite like a washing machine. This one's drum went back in much further, and it was almost like being a miner. (I appreciate every lump of coal I put on my fire so much more after this experience.) My face was only inches from the roof of this tunnel, and I was strapped in by my head, and was in up to my hips. I knew that I didn't like being shut in places, but it was a long time since I had felt the panic rising in the way I was experiencing. Usually I either avoided the situation or prepared myself for it.

I conveyed to the radiographer that I was beginning to panic, and she said as a parting shot: 'Oh you'll be fine, you've got the panic button,' and left closing the door behind her. I could feel my breathing getting faster and shorter, and the panic rising, as I realised I was at this person's mercy. This may sound dramatic, but just imagine your worst nightmare, and see how you feel! I did not appear to be going to get any understanding or support from this person, in fact I rather felt that I might get my leg slapped and be told to grow up, so I was thankful that I have cultivated a reflex, that when things get almost too much to cope with I go into auto-Reiki.

So that is what I did: I put my hands on myself, called for Reiki, and well . . . when the radiographer came back in, she had to speak twice to me to bring me back. I had managed to calm the panic and drift to somewhere wonderful. 'Good,' I thought, 'that's it, and I've come through.'

But this lady had not finished.

'Sorry we've got to take some again,' she said and disappeared again.

'I cannot believe this,' I thought, but still benefiting from the Reiki, I just turned it back on quickly before the panic slipped back in.

I was really pleased with myself, and very thankful for Reiki. But all was not over yet. The radiographer's wake up call was, 'We're just going to give you an injection.'

'Hang on a moment,' I thought, 'no one said anything

about injections. Not only that but what are they putting into me?'

I asked her this, and all she would say was, 'Nothing to worry about, it just shows us the blood vessels in the brain.'

'That's not what I asked,' I thought, but by this time she was already jabbing away.

I could feel the panic rising again, having injections is not among my favourite fun things to do. (Remember I am still strapped in and at *her* mercy.)

'Quickly, do some deep breathing, and some more Reiki and you'll be fine, she'll only be a moment.' Wrong again!

'Oh dear, I'll have to try the other side, this vein is no good.' (Rubbish! My veins are lovely, they always say so at the blood donor sessions!)

'Bend your arm please.' A large wad of cotton wool was shoved into the crook of my arm.

'Oh, this one hasn't gone right either, I'll need to get the doctor.' Another bale of cotton wool strategically placed, hindering any movement of my arms, unless I didn't mind bleeding all over the place.

By this time, if I wasn't strapped down, I'd have run out. In comes the doctor.

'Ah yes, your veins have given us some problems' – notice it is all my fault, I'm causing them problems, and I'm out-numbered two to one and trapped. That wasn't all. The doctor's resolution of this problem was to whack an injection into the back of my hand. I cannot tell you how I felt – I was having flash backs to the war films I had seen, *tie 'em down, inject, torture*. This may seem over-dramatic, but when fear and panic sets in, problems become really exaggerated.

Here I am gasping for air, and off they go 'Won't be much longer,' comes drifting back as they depart the room. Not much comfort. 'Reiki, Reiki, Reiki . . .' I'm saying to myself. 'Don't let the b—s get you.'

Well they didn't, and I have lived to Reiki another day.

A postscript to this episode made me smile – they lost the results! The next visit was fine – I sent Reiki ahead.

Fear of flying

I like my feet on the ground. I know that being able to transport large numbers of people in metal 'birds' at high speed through the air is a miracle, but it is one that I can live without. But when you promise to do something you have got to do it. I had promised Dorothy that as part of her Master training I would go and observe her First-Degree workshop and give feedback. The only way we could fit this into both our schedules was for me to fly from Scotland to Heathrow. The flight would only be around 1 hour 20 minutes. I have not flown for twenty-five years, and had no desire to do so. In fact I had a definite desire not to! But one's got to do what one's got to do, so off I went and I bought my ticket. For the next few weeks every time I came across it I got swarms of butterflies in my stomach. 'This is ridiculous. Statistics say it is a lot safer than driving up and down the motorways in a car.' (The alternative had the time been available.) This may be true, but I'm afraid I like my feet to be on the ground.

Anyway I set about preparing myself for this ordeal. I Reiki-ed the ticket, I Reiki-ed the fear thoughts, every time they popped up I turned on the Reiki. I can't say that just as I was boarding I didn't have a strong urge to run, but I got on the plane without stumbling, endured the journey – sitting next to two business men, who obviously were veteran flyers, and had no desire to chat. I admired the beauty of our planet, only visible in such a wide view from that height, and Reiki-ed like mad. I was glad to land, and gave thanks. I wonder if this is why the Pope kisses the ground when he arrives somewhere?

I spent a lovely few days with Dorothy and her First-Degree students, and was surrounded by enough Reiki to fly me home without the plane! However I did take the more conventional mode of transport. Despite a delay of nearly an hour and a half, I almost (but not quite) enjoyed the flight back. I Reiki-ed myself while I waited, and during the flight, and spent a fun time with a two year old watching the sunset, drawing and generally letting her climb all over me, much to her mum's delight. (Time is twice as long when you are that young.) I will not choose to fly again, but thanks to Reiki I managed it this twice.

From Phyl Parsons . . .
A vision

After taking my Reiki I, giving myself a treatment whilst resting on the spare room bed (which had been my mother's), I got a vision of a little girl with long blonde hair. This happened several times. Dorothy (my Reiki Master), thought it was a link back to my mother, and on looking out some old photographs, I'm sure it was my mother as a child who was visiting me.

From Senga Hodgson . . .
Relaxation and alertness

After my Reiki I initiation I felt so peaceful and awake and mellow, the best I have felt in a very long time. During the twenty-one days I gave myself treatments morning and evening. I find when I do this in the evening I'm asleep before I get to the last position and I always have a great sleep. When I wake up and give myself Reiki, I find I'm more alert and feel that I can take on the world!

From Britta Schlyter . . .
Find your Higher Self

Reiki for me is a wonderful contact with my Higher Self – our Lifestream. Whenever you feel low or depressed or have pain somewhere Reiki helps you. I often give myself Reiki and start it with about ten minutes of meditation to raise my vibrations. Then I feel myself *showered* in a golden/white light covering my whole body. To the tunes of Reiki Music Vol 4, I then give myself Reiki. I cannot describe in words the true feeling, but I will try. Reiki lifts you up to a higher dimension, your aching or sad body disappears and you become the spirit you once were before getting a body. You are no longer a body with a soul, but a soul with a body!

I haven't given Reiki to very many people, because here in Newtonmore people don't believe in it and are afraid of the unknown. Once I gave Reiki to an eight-year-old boy, who had been fighting. His little body was shaking and the tears running over his face. After fifteen minutes he was completely calm and happy, and he gave me a broad smile.

I have learnt one thing about Reiki – that your lifestyle is very important, I am mostly vegan with one exception – natural yoghurt. I drink little or no wine. I embrace positive thinking, outdoor exercise – such as walking in the forest or over the hills – whatever makes me feel good.

Distance healing

The most wonderful experience I ever had was being healed at a distance. In February '97 I had a stomach test at the Raigmore Hospital to see if I still had the bacteria that five months earlier had caused a perforated ulcer requiring a major operation with much pain afterwards. I told my wonderful Reiki Master Jennie Austin about it, and she said that when I had my appointment in the hospital she had a meeting with several other Masters and they would send me distant healing. They did! After the test all my pain, and with it the bacteria, had gone. I can never thank you all enough for my *miraculous* healing. God bless you all!

From Susan Coe . . .
Reiki treatment

I lay on the bed to receive a Reiki treatment from Jennie and Dorothy. Jennie put some beautiful relaxing music on and it drifted into my senses. Then hands were placed on me, a pair over my eyes, and another on my abdomen. It was a feeling of gentleness. Slowly I relaxed, my thoughts drifting with the music, deeper and deeper I went until at one point it felt as if my body turned to liquid, and gently melted into the bed, a wonderful sensation I had never experienced before. When my healing was over I didn't want to get up. I just lay relaxed and extremely happy. I was still on a high until I went to bed, and woke up the next day feeling great. Friends all said how good I was looking and that they could do with some of what I had been having, and when I get the chance I will certainly have some more!

From Jennie Austin . . .
First-Degree Reiki
There were no flashing lights, ringing bells or anything. In fact it was all very low key, in a cold room, with very little light shining in. The attunements had no visible effect on me at the time, nevertheless I took my Master's word for it that *something* had happened. However, over the next few days I noticed that my senses of smell and hearing were heightened, so much so that I could *smell* salt at a distance, and *hear* a pin drop on a carpet. I included Reiki in my life, but did not seem to get very much *proof* that it was working, as far as feelings were concerned. In hindsight I put this down to the fact that I was very stressed at the time. My sensitivity developed over the years, and I got the proof I searched for.

Second-Degree Reiki
Now this was totally different. I went with no expectations, and sat for my attunement, only to find that it was like sitting in a cinema watching a film in full Technicolor. Wow! I still have a hard time believing it, but I read my journal, and it is all there. During the following twenty-one days or so, I experienced a phenomenal amount of extra energy, and it seemed I could achieve anything that I set my mind to.

Third-Degree Reiki/Master training

After the wonderful experience of the Second-Degree training, and the super energy that I experienced following it, I
anticipated that the Master initiation would be something
equally mind-blowing, and probably even more so. I even
started to save jobs up that I thought would benefit from the
surge of enthusiasm and vitality. However I was to be disappointed. The attunement was very calming, no pictures, no
WOW at all. I felt let down. But in the days, weeks and years
that have followed there has been a gentle, subtle and extraor-
dinary series of happenings and experiences.

From Dorothy Berry-Lound . . .

First-Degree Reiki

I remember vividly my introduction to Reiki. There were
three of us in the class, and the others were ordinary just like
me. I had worried that the training might be a bit too new age
and spiritual for my tastes, but it was practical and down-to-
earth – and great fun! I didn't feel any different after the initiations and was amazed when my hands got hot and the Reiki
flowed. If I can do it anyone can.

Second-Degree Reiki

I had enjoyed my Reiki I class and looked forward a few
months later to Reiki II. I was not disappointed, finding the
initiation a wonderful experience and the benefits of being
able to use the distance healing symbol difficult to quantify.

Third-Degree Reiki/Master Degree training

I thought long and hard before commencing Master training. It
is a great responsibility and a considerable commitment both
in terms of time and money. I have not regretted it. My
training lasted officially for just over a year, but I find the
learning never stops – and my Master has become my best
friend.

From Ann Marie Davis . . .

First-Degree Reiki

I first had a one-off treatment of Reiki in December 1997, and I had to admit it was curiosity at first. I was overwhelmed by what I felt. There was heat and tingling in my hands, and I saw a steady flow of green mist passing in front of my eyes, and I could feel my blood flowing through my veins. I can't explain why I felt these things, but I can say that they had a profound effect on me. I needed to go further with Reiki and I wanted to know more. So I went to Jennie and went through my First Degree. Once again I had a very definite reaction. The one that had the biggest impact was in the form of regression, where I felt myself being transported to a time gone by where, from a height, I watched a little native American girl playing in a grassy field with trees behind her. Whilst watching her I began to realise that the little girl was me in another life.

It's very difficult to put Reiki into words, but since I found it I have become more confident and positive about myself and my life. Until now I have just flitted through life, with no purpose or direction.

The biggest impact of Reiki has been that I have just recently made a major decision about my life and I am uprooting, leaving my family and friends behind and I'm moving away to start a new life in another area. This is something I have always talked about, but have never had the confidence to go through with, until now. With the energy of Reiki I am now doing it and I am positive and confident that it's the right thing to do. Without Reiki there is no doubt in my mind that I would have stayed in the rut I've been in for the past fifteen years.

From the records of Jennie Austin

When I train people in Reiki, I ask that they send me a summary of their journal for the month after their initiation and some case studies. Here are few excerpts.

Moving house

On moving house – I'm positive that the Reiki has really helped me with the energy for the move, everything has gone so well, it's been quite amazing.

Stress

I'm really glad that I decided to take the Reiki course. I was rather anxious about going as I'm shy, but the benefits have been immeasurable. I've found Reiki to be of real help when I'm feeling stressed or run down – it has a very calming effect. In fact I would go so far as to say a Reiki treatment is like a meditation, especially so when you focus on what you are doing. I believe Reiki will help me along the road to personal fulfilment and development as well as healing aches and pains along the way.

T.L.C.

After the Reiki initiation weekend I continued to treat myself daily. I had just come out of a relationship and was in need of some T.L.C. to boost my spirit and heal my 'wounds'. The Reiki really helped to calm my mind, think clearer and also had the effect of creating a 'buffer zone' around my body so that I felt the calm no matter what the situation. Often it was the only way I could fall asleep at night without my mind racing – there were many nights I fell asleep with my hands at the base of my back!

Distance healing

We have been having very encouraging results with distance Healing on a lady who was verging on a nervous breakdown. Also an added bonus seems to be that her irritable bowel syndrome, from which she has suffered for over a year, seems at this time to be improving.

Hangovers

I had some good results with a male friend who had indigestion from too many beers!! After a quick treatment he was fine.

Practising Reiki

Weight loss

After regular treatments my husband has lost weight, (some of this has been up to him, but I think the Reiki has supported him), and he has been swearing less, and when he does he corrects himself without prompting from me!

Chronic fatigue syndrome

My partner has had chronic fatigue syndrome for at least nine years. It can get quite debilitating at times and he would ask for Reiki quite often. His body would be very achy and sore, his lymphatic system very full and his stomach and circulation 'stuck'. When treating him I could feel how much energy he was needing, depending on the area that was in most distress. Always, his stomach required a lot of work and afterwards he would be hungry. He usually fell asleep during the sessions and although they didn't immediately energise him, he felt more balanced and relaxed after each session.

Breathing difficulties

I treated a man who had breathing difficulties from the time he had farmer's lung, thirteen years ago, and again eighteen months ago. I had good results in that he has reduced his inhaler intake and his wife says he is much calmer around the home, and in general he says he feels better in himself and his breathing is much better.

Treating a sceptic

I first treated this lady in her mid-forties for toothache. I did two quite long sitting treatments on successive days. Her reaction was surprising in that she was quite sceptical at first. She commented on the difference in the temperature she felt as I went through the treatment, sometimes hot, at others very cool. She was able to sleep through the night for the first time since the pains had started and said the pain was less concentrated in the area than it had been previously. She came again asking for treatment for a muscle spasm in her shoulder and back, after a session in the gym. I treated her for three successive days for this. I did these treatments sitting on a beach in the sun! Again she found the intensity of the pain decreased immediately, as it dispersed away out through her body. She has asked for further treatments as a preventative measure – and that from a sceptic!

Children

From Jennie Austin
Distance healing for a tantrum!
My daughter lives 600 miles away, and so I was limited as to how much support I could give her when she had her first baby, Charlotte. Being able to send her Reiki when the need arose was a help, and made me feel a bit more supportive.

One day she phoned around four in the afternoon. Charlotte, who is very bright and energetic, was having her first tantrum.In fact she'd been having it since 10.00 am that morning. Toni was at her wit's end, having tried to cuddle, to divert, to be angry, to ignore it all. Nothing had stemmed the flow of Charlotte's performance. In moments of answering the call, and hearing the desperation in her voice, and the background sound effects from Charlotte I realised there was only one thing I could do. That was to send Reiki, using the distance healing. I did this while verbally offering comfort. There was suddenly a quiet in the back ground:

'You sent Reiki didn't you?'
'Yep!'
'Wish I'd phoned earlier.'
'Mmmm!'

Frustration
I called in to visit my friend, neighbour and fellow Reiki-ist. On arrival her toddler Colbyn was playing havoc, being

frustrated that his ability to walk did not match up to his desire. He was busily removing the books from shelves, coal from the hod, and in fact moving anything he could from his limited height, and getting very cross that he could not do more. Nothing appeared to appease him, and he got more and more frustrated the more she tried to help. She was tired too, and he was pushing his luck. Coming in from the calm of outside it was not hard to see what would help. I sat quietly on the sofa observing and sending some Reiki to them both. All the emotion calmed, and he ended by just sitting and playing with his toys, which moments before he had been very cross with. Cathleen and I had a cuppa, and a spent a very pleasant hour chatting before I left.

From Dorothy Berry-Lound . . .
Headache
Brett, a ten year old, boy, had a bad headache. His mum asked if I could do anything for him. With the help of Reiki the headache was fixed, and the child went to sleep sitting bolt upright – all within five minutes. His mum asked if I could go and live with her!

Animals

From Jennie Austin . . .
Animals are wonderful subjects for Reiki. They do not have hidden agendas, they just want to be well, and they are past Masters at recognising something that is pleasurable.

An elderly spaniel
The day that I was initiated to the Second Degree, I phoned Jane, who lives about 600 miles away. She said, 'What are you on? It's pouring out of the phone this end!' After I had explained to her that I had just done my Second Degree and that I could now do Reiki distance healing, she asked if I would treat her rescued King Charles Spaniel called Mimmy.

Mimmy was elderly, blind, deaf and arthritic, and spent all her time either eating or sleeping. She was a perky little soul when she was awake, but Jane was concerned that she was not having much of a life, and her arthritis was causing her discomfort. I sent her Reiki that evening, and early next morning there was a phone call saying that Mimmy had got up, walked out on to the veranda to observe the other dogs as they played in the garden, and was taking a real interest in life. I sent her top up treatments from then on, and she lived the rest of her life with more involvement and less discomfort.

Paralysis

I have three dogs, two of them are sisters and both were born with deformities. One day when I got home, Inka, who is normally full of beans, appearing to be a cross between a meerkat and a kangaroo rather than a dog, came to greet me in a sorry state, dragging her back legs. I was concerned because her spine has a twist in it, and also I had found a tic attached to her previously. I took her to the vet in case there was something amiss with her back or that she had contracted Lyme Disease (I was worried about the tic – Lyme disease is passed on by them and it affects the nervous system). The vet manipulated her to see if anything was wrong with her back, and gave her a shot of antibiotics, saying that he couldn't find anything clinically wrong, but if she had not improved by the morning to bring her back, and he would have her in for observation and investigation. I went home and Reiki-ed her, and within the hour she was bouncing around looking much happier and more her old self. We had no recurrences.

Back pain

Tawni her sister has a worse deformity; she too has a twist in her spine, but also one of her legs is malformed and shorter, so this puts extra strain on her back. Because she is a game little tot, she tends to join in and rough house with the other dogs, and runs through the heather as though she has four good legs. Sometimes she gets it wrong and this causes her pain. She has painkillers from the vet, but I only use these in extreme cases as usually Reiki sorts the pain out. Most days she gets a treatment and extra if she has strained herself. She can be quite pushy when she wants a treatment!

Spinx

I also have Spinx who is thirteen. She nearly died nine years ago, after a vet made a mess of her spaying before I took her on. Along with excellent veterinary care and Reiki she survived. She still has problems resulting from the initial problem, but on a recent check up at our vets he said that she was good for a dog of nine, let alone thirteen. She runs with the pups (who are now four years old!) and is very active, and can be quite demanding when it comes to going out for walks etc. She too asks for her Reiki treatments and she wants them *now*!

All three of my dogs have to be shut away, if Reiki is going on, as they all want to take a share. After the treatment is finished and they are let out, the first place they run to is the room were it has been going on.

Stunned birds

As we live in the middle of nature, we get a lot of wildlife frequenting our patch. This includes a wide variety of birds. This is lovely, but they do not seem to see windows. Several times a year we will hear a thump, and then on rushing outside find a little body stunned and somewhat shocked. A few minutes of Reiki and they are perking up, and ready to fly. I usually top them up with distance healing until I feel they no longer need it. Sometimes we are able to recognise them, and keep an eye on their progress as they feed at our table.

Wild animals

Living in the Highlands of Scotland we see lots of animals, some domesticated and some wild, many of which are unapproachable, and a few who are obviously hurt. Distance healing Reiki enables me to help even the most inaccessible of animals.

Fear and aggression

At one time I had my own dog grooming business. Some dogs on their first visit would be apprehensive and even aggressive in their fear of the unknown. I found that offering Reiki was a lovely way to put them at their ease, and to associate me not just with the sometimes unpleasant experience of having their knots and tangles dealt with, but also with something that supported them in these ordeals and made them feel good. After their first Reiki visit, they were usually eager to come in, much to their owners chagrin – not even a backward glance in many cases!

From Dorothy Berry-Lound . . .

Vomiting

My cat Juju kept vomiting and her stomach was swollen. I offered her Reiki and she lifted herself up so that I could Reiki her stomach. Some 20 minutes later she asked to go out and it was obvious her bowels were kick-started. No more sickness and back to her old self, so no need for a trip to the vet this time.

From Ann Marie Davis . . .

Relaxation

After I had been initiated to the First Degree of Reiki, my dog Tinker was very uneasy about what I was doing and wouldn't settle for long, he also couldn't look me in the eye. I wanted to try and get him to unwind and sit quietly occasionally, because he is very extrovert and active all the time. After a couple of days he slowly started to lie down beside me and allow me to give him Reiki for ten to fifteen minutes at a time.

He always fell into a deep sleep which would last for 20 to 30 minutes, giving him rest and me peace! I also used it a lot on him just after he had had an operation. He wasn't very well and his whole body shivered continuously. I would sit with him, giving him Reiki for just five minutes and he'd stop shivering and his breathing would ease and he'd fall into a good sleep. He is now up and about as normal, he's not been sick again and his wound is healing quickly.

Animal case studies by Jennie's students

Here are some case studies that have been sent in by students for their initiations.

Patient: Sixteen-hand mare, 17 years old
Problem: lame

This mare was lame due to tendosynovitus in her rear right-hand leg, and was thus rather out of condition. I brought her in and groomed her and then gave her Reiki for about 40 minutes. She was very well-behaved during the Reiki, although a little curious as to what I was doing. The human hand positions do not really apply to a horse – it is difficult to get them to lie on their backs! So I just worked my way down her sides from head to tail and then treated her bad leg. I treated her again two days later for a further 40 minutes, and she fell asleep, so she obviously didn't object. I gave her another treatment five days later for 40 minutes when there had been a slight improvement in her lameness. I repeated the treatment again and there was again an improvement. She still has trouble picking her feet up to be shod, however her general condition has improved and her limp has all but disappeared.

Patient: a mare
Problem: aggressive behaviour and bad temperament

I picked this horse for my case study because in the last year she has become a bit difficult to handle when out away from the 'herd'. I was interested to see what effects Reiki would have on her overall temperament and disposition. The first treatment consisted of going out for a hack around the surrounding area. I had been finding that she was unwilling to go forward around the whole hack, often stopping, backing up and occasionally threatening to rear. I laid one hand on her withers and one near her rump and walked around the area. Although she did stop at first there was no aggression and I simply sat, used Reiki and waited until she moved on. We got around the whole hack with as many stops but fewer fights.

The second treatment followed the form of the first, only this time I only used one hand on her withers area. There was a lot of heat generated between the two of us, and watching her I noticed that she was more alert and her disposition had improved. She stopped less and even when she did she was interested in what was going on around her, and there was no fight between us. I feel that as I am using Reiki I am calmer within and as she is receiving it she calms and seems to realise that there is no requirement to fight, go backwards, etc. The whole hack was improved by the change in the aggressive behaviour and I kept my hand on her withers area for most of the walk.

The third treatment didn't go so well due to *my* disposition! She reverted back to a more aggressive stance and although I used Reiki on her I was less calm within myself and I think this affected her too.

For the fourth treatment I decided to try an 'on the ground' treatment, before I rode out. I worked on her neck and head area, back and legs. She seemed very relaxed and dozed off at points. It takes quite a long time to Reiki a whole horse so I completed the treatment during the hack. She was much improved compared with the previous treatment, as was I. I feel there is a general improvement. She appears happier and more relaxed, there is less tension in her neck area. My demeanour seems to have improved as well!! I know also that she has fairly stiff joints in one leg as a result of an old injury, so I worked this area after the hack.

I decided to work on the ground for the final treatment for this study. She seems to enjoy the hands-on treatment and certainly relaxes, even if she starts off taking an aggressive stance, she seems to back off by the end of the treatment. I worked for some time around her neck and leg area. I certainly hope to continue the treatments beyond this study and I need to ensure that I make time to do this as her whole attitude seems to have improved in general as has mine towards her.

Patient: a boxer dog ten years old.
Problem: A sore ear after an operation to open up his ear and remove a polyp. He also has a slight heart murmur.

I did my Reiki half way through my dog's recovery and started treating him regularly as soon as I could. His energy levels improved after his ordeal. He knew a good thing when he found it, and would not leave my side in the mornings until he had had his Reiki treatment, refusing to budge, much to his dad's surprise as he is normally well behaved. I gave him 20 minutes during which time he was very quiet and still. When I had finished I told him to go to his bed, which he did immediately, and promptly fell asleep!! After further treatments the ear healed well, with little scarring. He likes his treatments early in the day rather than later on. He heads for me first thing and sits there not moving while he gets his Reiki, and looks as though he is in cloud cuckoo land, with a look of utter bliss on his face. We were astounded at the speed of his recovery with the Reiki. He still insists on his morning treatments!

Reiki can help with all sorts of visits to the vet's, especially pre- and post-operatively. Before an operation they are not allowed to eat – for what to them must seem like ages – then they are taken from their family to somewhere strange, and then all sorts of unpleasant and unfamiliar things happen, and then often they experience pain! Reiki can help all the way through, especially the distance healing, to offer them comfort when in a strange and 'hostile' (as far as they are concerned) environment.

Plants

Plants love Reiki, and repay a little care with beauty and abundance.

From Jennie Austin . . .

Cuttings

When I went south to do the Bach flower remedies training course, I stayed in a guest house where they had a magnificent wax plant. When I left, Pam and Ernie gave me two cuttings with strict instructions of what to do to propagate them into equally magnificent plants. These poor cuttings had to go to my Mum's for a visit and then a 600 mile journey home during some of the hottest weather on record. I duly followed the instructions I had been given. Nothing! 18 months later they were still there and not even a root had appeared. I didn't throw them out because they were still green. I then decided to Reiki them. Within days tiny roots appeared, and now I have two magnificent plants which are full of flowers during the summer.

Sprouts

I do quite a bit of sprouting seeds, e.g. alfalfa, mung beans, mustard and cress, as they are a cheap and healthy way of getting vitamins and fresh greens. I Reiki them for just a few minutes a day and in so doing the growing time is much shorter, they also grow more sturdy. I have done experiments with a control jar full, and the difference in the speed of growth and their vitality is really noticeable.

Reviving 'dead' plants

I have a friend who thinks I am a plant rescue and sanctuary. At one time she would be forever turning up with dying plants that she had *rescued* from the local supermarket. She would say that she just couldn't leave them there, so she had bought them, and brought them round to me to make better. Apart from a few which were really past it we managed to revive them, and they went on to give seasons of pleasure.

Epilogue

I recall the reason that I accepted the invitation to write this book – it was my desire to provide Reiki with an opportunity to reach those that would not otherwise come into contact with it. It was not to provide me with the opportunity to shine as a writer!

This book was conceived and birthed in a very short time. I threatened to write a book for some time, but put it off, because so many others were covering the subject so well. I was then offered the chance to write a book that would not necessarily be a masterpiece, but that would make the fact that Reiki existed accessible to many. I just couldn't say no.

I hope that I have written an accessible book and that the light of Reiki will shine through my limitations as an author for you to see, and that it will touch you in some way or another.

Acknowledgements

As with any project there are many who support, aid and encourage the person up front. During this short pregnancy there have been so many that I am wary of leaving anyone out, but despite making this sound like a speech from an Oscar Winner I would like to mention just a few, and those that are not mentioned in name will know who they are and that Reiki and I thank them too.

I thank:
Mike for creating the space for me to eat, sleep and breath nothing but book.

Practising Reiki

Anne Keltie for my First-Degree initiation, and Cathleen for nudging me along my path with Reiki, June for her wisdom and kindness as my Reiki Master (Second and Third Degrees) and dear friend, Dorothy and Alice for their special friendship, support, enthusiasm, confidence, suggestions and practical assistance, and for being my computer helplines along with Keith Harris. To Jane my soul-sister, to Nisby for setting me on the route of my life path so many years ago, and to Vera, a friend indeed, for grounding and honest counsel and support.

Thank you to the many Masters who have been generous in sharing their visions of Reiki with me and from whom I have learnt much, and to all of the Reiki-ists who have chosen me to birth them into Reiki, and have shared their experiences with me, as well as all the Reiki-ists who have given input to this venture, especially those who have sent me distance healing to keep my energies up, it certainly worked!

Thanks to my patients who have enabled me to experience Reiki in such a variety of ways.

Thanks to Keith Whittles who contacted me.

Thank you to the musicians and actors whose talents lifted my spirits, energised and inspired me while I became familiar with the intricacies of a certain computer system, or just needed a break and time to focus.

Special thanks to Spinx, Inka and Tawni, my girls, who have kept me company throughout, and reminded me of the need to take time out and to eat!

To Edward and friends for their help and humour and to Alan for making the connection with them! Thank you.

And of course, thank you Reiki.

May you all experience the blessings of Reiki,

Jennie Austin

Recommended Reading

Reiki

Frank Arjava Petter, *Reiki Fire*. Lotus Light, Shangri La, 1997. ISBN 0-914955-50-0

Frank Arjava Petter, *Reiki – The Legacy of Dr Usui*. Lotus Light, Shangri La, 1998 ISBN 0-914955-56-X

William Lee Rand, *Reiki – The Healing Touch, First and Second Degree Manual*. Southfield, MI, Vision Publications. ISBN 0-9631567-0-5

Karyn Mitchell, *Reiki – A Torch in Daylight*. Mind River Publications, 1994. ISBN 0-9640822-1-7

Chakras

Shalila Sharamon and Bodo J. Baginski, *The Chakra Handbook*, Lotus Light Publications. ISBN 0-941524-85-X

Naomi Ozaniec, *The Chakras*. Element, 1997. ISBN 1-86204-029-X

C. W. Leadbeater, *The Chakras*. Wheaton Illinois Theosophical Publishing House, 1977. ISBN 0-8356-0422-5

Blawyn and Jones, *Chakra Workout*. Llewellyn Publications, 1996. ISBN 1-56718-074-4

Barbara Ann Brennan, *Hands of Light*. Bantam New Age. ISBN 0-553-34539-7

Miscellaneous

Bearing All in Umbria – The Diary of Toby Bear, real stories from a bear in Italy, Dorothy Berry-Lound. Minerva.

Keith Harris's recommended reading

Dr Ayn W. Cates, *Consider This – Recovering Harmony and Balance Naturally.* Findhorn

Jenny Cole, *Journeys (With Cancer).* Pawprints

Dr Richard Gerber, *Vibrational Medicine: New Choices for Healing Ourselves.* Bear & Co

Clare G. Harvey and Amanda Cochrane, *Vibrational Healing.* Thorsons.

Matthew Manning, *No Faith Required.* Eikstein

Harry Oldfield and Roger Coghill, *The Dark Side of the Brain: Major Discoveries in the Use of Kirlian Photography and Electro-crystal Therapy.* Element

Dr Christine Page, *Beyond the Obvious.* C. W. Daniel